Rampage and Revenge

Bigfoot: Renegade

Misty Allabaugh

Illustrations of "RED" were done by Kimberly Goss-Kearney.

Books in the Bigfoot Series

Book One

Flesh and Fury

Bigfoot: Rogue

Book Two

Rampage and Revenge

Bigfoot: Renegade

Coming Soon

Book Three

Brutality and Betrayal

Bigfoot: Rebel

Dedication

For my mom and dad. . .

I have always known that no matter what I do or where my travels have taken me, I've always had a place to come home to. It has been this guidance and unconditional love that has shown me how truly blessed I am to have parents that simply wanted the best for me. Whatever made me happy was their ultimate goal.

Looking back I see the sacrifices they made, how hard they worked so my brother and I could always have the very best. It is with this thought in mind that I would like to thank them. As parents, they would always say there was no greater joy in life than to see their children healthy and happy. I can't remember the number of times they extended this joy to include others, opening their home, and often their wallets, to ensure that if they were able, no one should have a want or need.

I am so fortunate and lucky to have had two parents such as you; you have been my inspiration, my guiding light, my shoulders to cry on, and my best friends. I am so excited, and it is with great honor that I dedicate this book to my now retired father, Ed, and the memory of my wonderfully sweet mama. Thank you both from the very depths of my being.

She May Be Gone, but Never Forgotten

Mary Elizabeth Allabaugh

July 23, 1953- December 23, 2007

Forward

It is with great pleasure that I bring you book two in the Bigfoot series. I hope you enjoy the story that unfolds in the pages to come. You are about to meet a new character who I hope you will love just as much as you did Mari. As an author, it has been my intention to mix fact with fiction and stir in a healthy dose of pure fantasy for fun!

It was also my intention to show that women today can be strong and courageous yet remain feminine and flirty. We are tough and have the ability to face the greatest challenges head on and do it with courage and strength of character. No longer do we have to sacrifice our morals or who we are as women to get the job done.

We are single mothers, professional career women, survivors of domestic violence, and yes, even authors who stay up late at night to write horror novels! We are not only a stronger generation, but we are a new and empowered one that I personally am proud to be a part of.

I've been on an incredible personal journey, and through its trials and triumphs I have found my wings and learned to fly again. It is my hope that you can too.

Kate Mitchell is a woman who I think embodies all of these ideals yet has her own gift to add to the mix. It is this gift that puts an edgy twist on what could potentially become a tired, done, and did Bigfoot series! Along with Kate, there will be some faces you will recognize, and an old relationship will become new again.

I hope you enjoy the story as much as I enjoyed writing it for you!

Prologue

A chill swept over her. . .it was time.

Kate was ready for battle. She didn't need the tiny shift in the air or the silence of the forest to warn her that she was no longer alone. Kate had the upper hand, the edge. She felt him.

The hatred that oozed from the beast was palpable, and she could smell it as easily as a dog could smell fear. There was no fear in Kate. She was strong and focused, determined. It was game on.

The truth was it didn't take a genius or a shift in the wind to know these woods held secrets she didn't need to see to know existed. Of course, the smell had given the creature away long before the wind shifted. A pungent cross between rotting road kill and wet dog together rolled in shit. Combined, it produced an odor that once you smelled it, you never forgot.

All of these were just bonuses to Kate, helpful but not needed. Her strength lay within her mind, and she was prepared to sacrifice it and her life to end Kretha's path of carnage.

Kretha, once a mighty Chief to his Clan of Leviathans, was her purpose for being here; there was a debt to repay, and revenge would be hers. She cleared her mind and turned to face her challenger. He'd told her he was coming. To see her nemesis brought a grin as maniacal and ugly as that of the creature to her face.

It was at this moment that Kate knew two things: the battle lines had long past been drawn, and today was going to be a damn good day for killing. She had, after all, warned him, had she not?

Dylan Thomas's voice echoed in her head, "Breathe, Kate, focus on nothing but your target and let your shot go." She grinned again.

The serenity of the forest was broken by automatic gunfire. . .

Chapter One

September

What was supposed to be an adventure was turning into a disaster. Who went camping and forgot the toilet paper? Everyone had a list; how hard was it to pack the items on your assigned list? This camping trip into Montana's back woods was not a big deal; everyone had their own ATV, each person was responsible for his or her own things, and it was past time some of these so-called "outdoors people" had to figure it out for themselves

Maybe a couple times using the foliage to wipe with would allow the mighty campers to pull their heads out of their newly leaf-wiped asses and get it together.

Kate Mitchell was a hard ass and knew her business; she also knew that this was going to be a long week. So far, today, she'd discovered that no one had brought extra fuel for the ATVs or any matches. There was one forgotten sleeping bag, and now one genius had misplaced their toilet paper. It would be easier to understand if it was just one person being irresponsible, but so far, three out of the eight people had each misplaced or flat out forgotten items. And one of the offenders was Kate's own employee; she was seriously pissed.

Sometimes Kate wondered if guiding these trips was worth the pay. Admittedly, however, riding an ATV around the mountains was one of her favorite past times. Camping, fishing, and in general, being in the outdoors was what she lived for.

This summer, however, was one like no other: the people were ruder and expected five-star services on a wilderness adventure. Everyone registered months before their individual trips, and each person in the party was sent a specific list of what to pack as far as clothing and food, right down to the amount of toilet paper that would be required for a five-day, back-country ATV tour.

The brochures clearly said this was an outdoor adventure. Sure, they usually did whatever it took to please the customer, but enough was enough!

Kate paused and looked to the mountains; why was she still doing this? Maybe it was time to do something else, go somewhere and be someone else. She'd spent years guiding, and it was time to take herself on an adventure. Let someone else worry about making her comfortable for a change. Right. That wasn't going to happen—you didn't walk away from the family business.

In all honesty, she didn't give a crap about these people anymore, but she did care about her family, and this is what they did. *Hell*, she thought, her attitude really sucked.

It had been a trying couple years after her mom died, the family drifted in a sea of bills, depression, and boredom. One spring, Kate, her brother, Jace, their dad, and nephew had loaded up the old ATVs and went riding. It was the beginning of an obsession; and before long the idea to guide back-country ATV adventures was dreamt up. A year spent saving to buy a few extra machines, pay off many of those bills, apply for all the guiding licenses and special permits was all it took. The ball was rolling.

In those early days, Kate, her dad, and Jace guided the tours together, each taking two people. Soon word got out, and it wasn't long before it became necessary for each of them to guide separate tours with the help of another guide.

Unfortunately, Kate's "helper" this year was the greenhorn. Rich was a good kid, but he was young and lazy. He had until this trip was done in five days to pull it together, or he would move on to be some other company's mistake. Kate couldn't help but wonder if Rich was short for Richard Cranium, aka Dick Head. The thought made her grin.

This tour had five clients, two guides, and one cook and so far, two clients and her greenhorn were the ones to forget their gear. Keeping the ATVs running was Kate and the other guide's responsibility. Forgetting the extra fuel was inexcusable and embarrassing.

Kate had radioed camp, and luckily, Blake hadn't left with the food trailer and was able to bring it along. Blake was responsible, and Kate knew she could count on her chief bottle washer and cook.

When Blake got up to the lake, there would be eight people total. Typically, there were a few fisherman out and about this time of year, and maybe a few hunters, but it was early fall, and so far they had seen no one. As predicted, it had rained last night, and that kept the dust down. The forecast called for clear skies, so the hope was for the group to spend today traveling the ten miles off road to Grizzly Lake, spend the afternoon setting up camp, and by evening everyone would be so tired that there would be no need for further entertainment.

Days two, three, and four were spent fishing for the Arctic Graylings and trout, hiking, taking photos, or basically whatever the group wanted. After all, it was their dime. On one of the days, they would ride another mile farther up the canyon to Sylvia Lake and spend the day fishing and glassing the avalanche chutes for bears and other animals.

On the fifth day, they broke camp and traveled back to the launch area where everyone, exhausted but exhilarated from the mountain air, got into their rented four-wheel drives and drove themselves back to Kalispell. If they were smart, they had a standing hotel reservation that included use of a hot tub. What they did after they left wasn't Kate's problem, and again, she just couldn't care less.

****

In the beginning, Big Sky Adventures had done everything for the customers, all they had to do was pack their personal possessions and sit on the machine; if they couldn't ride, a special trailer with seats was provided. All the client had to do was watch the scenery go by, and some folks actually preferred that.

Kate, Jace, and her dad fixed the food, cleaned up the camp, and catered to every whim. After a year, it became clear that most people wanted the "wilderness adventure," so it was decided to try a season of getting them safely to the lake and making sure the bears didn't eat them. For the most part, they were on their own.

They'd made a few adjustments here and there, but ultimately, it worked as Big Sky Adventures had only a handful of rules. The first was absolutely no alcohol: if you brought it, you were done and sent on your way with no refund. If you were a guide and so much as thought about it, you were done.

The second was safety at all costs: each guide was armed and well trained in how to use a gun against a wild animal. Clients and guides were all required to wear helmets and eye protection. Literally, it was not brain surgery, but there was always the one person who just didn't get it.

The final rule was simple: after you got off a machine, the first thing you did was refuel. The machines needed to be ready at a moment's notice. And damn it anyway if that little shit Rich didn't just break rule three, who forgets the gas? A greenhorn, that's who. It was pointless to be annoyed—it was what it was—and what it was, was a giant cluster. What could Kate do? Deal with it and move on, that's what.

****

The Leviathans from across the mountains had spent the early summer watching the humans on the Noise

Makers. They had hidden in the trees and covered their smell as Khryl had told them to.

The female that the Chief had sent them to protect didn't know of his presence, but Rooba always knew when she was near. The mighty giant sensed something powerful within her, but he was sent to watch over the Clan who hid deep within the high mountains. They seemed peaceful, but again Rooba felt darkness emanating from their Chief.

He knew the Chief to be named Kretha and reported to his own Clan, even though the one called Kretha spent many hours watching the female, he did not seem to be a threat.

Rooba was glad to return to his own side of the mountains when Khryl called him and the other hunters home.

****

The Clan's presence from the other side of the mountain went unnoticed by Kate. No one knew at the time, but the beast known as Kretha was realizing the humans were invading his beloved mountain. Had he known the pleasure it would bring, his lust for blood and wrath would have begun months earlier. He'd soon experience euphoria by stalking his way through the forest.

Killing everything and everyone in his path, leaving a trail of bodies and destruction.

Chapter Two

Blake arrived with the trailer filled with five days' worth of food for eight people, and after dinner was prepared, everyone assisted by helping haul the food to the bear-proof containers that were cached well away from the camp. They'd never had a bear problem until earlier this year, but it wasn't called Grizzly Lake because the name was cute.

Regardless, better safe than sorry. Earlier, on a June trip, they had returned from the upper Moose Valley on day three to find that the food was fine, but the camp had been raided; one tent was collapsed, and the fire pit destroyed.

The guides had taken turns through the night keeping watch, and by morning things were back to normal. Oddly enough, they never saw the bear that did it, or any bears for that matter. Another source of discontent among many of her clients was the lack of bears that were out this year. As if she could control where the bears went.

In Kate's mind, it was just something else for them to bitch about.

Thinking about it now, Kate had wondered about the lack of bears this season. She'd seen one little black bear when they'd come up before clients this spring to clear blow down and prep the trail. Not one had been spotted on the slides all season, and it was definitely strange, but there was nothing she could do about it, and if she was honest, she preferred not to have to worry about them raiding her camp.

Now that the work was done, the fire was blazing, and everyone had eaten, it was time to relax. This was the usual time that she and the guides got to know the clients, all thoughts of raided camps and lack of predators was quickly forgotten.

****

Typically it was families, groups of friends, or coworkers that came on the trips. There were three senior guides. These included Kate, Jace, and their dad, Tom. Kate always guided into Grizzly Lake; it was supposed to be a relaxing trip that was, in general, mostly about camping and fishing.

Jace guided a trip that followed the river in the valley that specialized in fly fishing. Dad typically guided the easier trips; he enjoyed doing the trail rides that had just a few people in the group, they camped at three different spots on a thirty-mile, five-day journey.

Kate got the families, Tom got the older people seeking fresh air, and Jace got the single men wanting to fish. There was no justice in that, and Kate grinned as she remembered trying to fight her way into guiding the river trip. As she remembered it, she was told something along the lines of, "Shit outta luck, Sis," at the time; she was seriously offended even though she owned the company.

In the end it was about success, and she had to be honest, fly fishing was great, but in small doses, and especially this year there might have been bloodshed with some of the idiots that signed up for Jace's trips.

Kate knew her patience was shot, but, luckily, hunting season was around the corner. Hunting was all about family, no clients, and no pressures. Archery, simply put, was a crisp, cold fall morning, a bow and arrow, and if the heavens were willing, a bugling bull answering the challenge for his hierarchy. That month and a half made the world go round; well actually, it made the other ten and a half bearable.

As the day caught up to her, Kate looked around at the group; this would be the last one for the year. Even though it was early September, you could never tell when a winter storm would dump three feet of snow at these elevations, so after this, it was time to pack it up until next year.

Other than Richard Cranium, who didn't know shit, and Blake, the other five people in the group, Kate suspected, were relatively inexperienced in the ways of camping. She glanced around quickly, and her gaze fell on the young couple. They acted like they had a clue, and she was still on the fence as to their experience, but the others were laughable. Mostly, Kate just felt sorry for the little girl.

The family rode the four wheelers well enough, but that is where their skill ended. She searched her mind for a second and recalled that they were from Colorado. Jeff was a contractor and mom, Radka, who spoke with a distinct Russian accent, was most likely president of the PTO. She thought she was the cat's meow, and every red-blooded human would have to have been a fool not to notice her fake chest enhancements. They were, after all, clearly on display, and Kate had caught "The Cranium," as she was now calling him, ogling her. It would appear; however, that Radka was not enjoying the smoke from the fire, the giant mosquitoes, or the prospect of several nights in a tent. Their daughter was cute but not old enough to ride on her own, so she partnered up with her dad and looked to be having the time of her life. Kate was pretty certain her name was Marley.

Jeff, Radka (speaking of weird names, really?), and Marley seemed like the perfect little family from Colorado. Usually her first opinions were good, she figured Radka was going to be a problem or eventually have something to gripe about. During introductions she was quick to point out that "everyone can just call me Rad."

Kate couldn't help but wonder if that was in some way an implication of Rad thinking she was completely chill and totally "radical."

Frankly, she was a joke. How long was she going to be able to keep up the perfect hair and makeup routine? Again, that was a no-brainer. The answer was until Kate reminded her—as she did almost every female—that makeup and hair crap attracted bears. It brought Kate much joy to explain that when bears came, bad things happened and that you would not need makeup and hair essentials once said bear ate your face off. Evil, she knew, but it was stated in the brochure to not bring it into the back country. However, she could count on one hand how many times a "lady" of Rad's "class" actually followed the directions. Yup, probably just conjecture, but the missus was not going to be fun.

It might have just been Kate's overall bitchiness, but Jeff looked like a creeper, and she'd bet he was hiding something. She didn't like him and certainly didn't trust him. He was probably a rich asshole who had affairs right and left and thought his financial status made it okay to cheat on his wife. Again it was conjecture, but Kate would be damned if she'd turn her back on him.

Next up was the young couple; they'd told her that this was their official engagement trip, whatever the hell that meant. They looked to be mid-twenties, colossally fit, and in all honesty, beautiful people. Ben was tall, dark, and hot; Mimi was perky, and Kate detected a little Native in her. She hid it under some beautiful hair that surprisingly had strips of pink in it. Kate liked her immediately, and if she wasn't so damn nice, Kate would have stereotyped her into the Triple B group: big-boobed/blond/bimbo.

She liked them though; they weren't afraid to refuel their machines, and they'd set up their own tent. Neither one had forgotten anything on the list, a definite plus in Kate's book. Ben and Mimi might make the trip bearable, fun even. She still didn't understand an engagement trip though. Who does stuff like that? Kate might have joked about Mimi's name as she had done with Radka's, but Mimi was French for Mary, and that was Kate's mom's name, and that pink hair showed some attitude; she liked it.

Kate was tired and not just physically. This year had been difficult, and she had no idea why. She always told herself that when it stopped being fun, it was time to get out. If only it was that easy.

It was the norm that the guides waited until the campers went to bed before they did, but tonight she was going to leave Blake to handle it. The Cranium wouldn't be in charge of anything, she decided. The idiot couldn't find his own ass in the dark.

Standing, she told the campers good night and made eye contact with a surprised Blake. She merely nodded at him and went to her tent. She was just done. Why did her head ache so badly?

Before flopping fully dressed onto her sleeping bag, Kate checked that her shotgun was loaded and her pack was inside the tent. Even nearing exhaustion, it was foolish to let your guard down in the mountains. Being bear bait was not how she wanted to end the year.

Chapter Three

The beast hid among the trees, silent and ever watchful. His kind had been in this area for a long time. They had encountered many of the humans before and had no problems scaring them away. This particular group of humans was led by a female, her scent stronger than the others. He had smelled her on many occasions and was confused as to why she continued to come into the area with all the humans. They came with their loud machines.

Some of them invariably rode the Noise Makers up the valley closer to his Clan, and this was always a worry. It was unspoken but simply known that humans were to be avoided at all costs. Last year the Clan had moved down the mountain when the drought had come, but another Clan had also come to the area. The Clans did not war with one another, but it was again an unspoken rule that you coexist. They tolerated one another. The Clan that came, however, brought death and destruction. They also brought many humans to a land where the Gods were already angry and throwing the great fire.

The beast knew that the Clan was again living several mountains over, and he was certain that they had broken the code of the mighty Leviathans. He had seen humans with the other Clan; he had witnessed the humans playing with the cubs! It was unheard of and against the Leviathan's Law. There was no one to care, though, and they kept to their side of the mountains.

In his Clan, he was Chief; his word and will was always done. He was known as Kretha, and his mate was Ravana; together they had two cubs, Goya and Kali. He did not like the females of his Clan, and that included his mate and cub, Kali. He ruled his Clan with an iron fist, and none dared break the rules. He was grooming Goya to take his position as Chief one day, even if that day would be a long time coming.

He centered his attention back to the humans that had again invaded his home. His hunters and watchers had tried to scare them away several suns ago but to no avail.

The humans did not seem to be a problem, but Kretha was too proud to allow them to stay. His hunters were already questioning why he had allowed the humans to remain. If he did not scare them away on this moon, he would look like a fool to his Clan.

The mighty beast shrank back into the bushes in silence. The humans with their loud machines and Pain Sticks had no idea he lurked so close. His ability to escape detection was a source of great pride.

Kretha would return later; he would bring Goya and another trusted hunter, together they would remove the threat just as they had always done.

The Chief snarled as a memory from long ago surfaced: two men had come into the Clan's territory and resisted their warnings. Kretha suspected that the men had spotted them, but he and his warriors had chased them

from the mountain, and they had not returned.

****

Kate couldn't sleep; the sounds from the campers had slowly faded as one by one, they retired for the night. She could hear the crackle of the fire and occasionally some birds or bugs that she rather not know about making noises in the trees. She could also hear something else; was someone still awake and walking around?

Usually the sounds of the forest were a comfort, but tonight she was restless; maybe it was the stress of the day or the fact she was beyond exhausted. She lay there and listened; someone was definitely still awake. It was probably Blake, but she had better be sure. There was a kid on this trip, and the last thing she needed was a lost eight-year-old on her watch.

Kate, still fully dressed, stepped from her tent and was surprised by the stillness of the forest; there wasn't anyone awake, but she was certain she'd heard footsteps. Not turning her back to the night, she reached into her tent for the loaded shotgun; it was modified and the tube held extra rounds. She rotated buckshot with slugs. It wrought more destruction, and she had no problems using the gun. She was, in fact, quite good with it and handled it with ease.

The fire was dying, there were no flames to light up the clearing, but over the years she'd found that you didn't always need light; she crouched low in the shadows and controlled her breathing. She listened, watched, and waited. The wait wasn't long; something was walking just inside the trees out of her line of sight. It circled the camp and had it not been for the occasional snap of a twig underfoot, it would have moved silently. This was a little disconcerting for Kate; bears made noise, and deer and elk would not circle the camp, they would avoid it.

Kate felt fairly certain that she had not been detected and clicked the safety off the gun. There were stirrings in the other tents as their occupants rolled over and moved around, but everyone was asleep. Blake and The Cranium shared a tent, but it was on the opposite side of the clearing. A little reinforcement would have been nice, but something told her to remain motionless. Besides, there was no doubt the greenhorn would panic and go bat-shit crazy; the idea of him with a loaded gun was scarier than whatever lurked in the trees.

It seemed like hours, but it was in fact, only minutes before whatever was inside the timber moved off. Kate listened and again was certain that it was a person walking around. A person familiar with the area would be able to move quietly; could it be that Holy Roller preacher Darrell again?

He'd caused some problems, complaining about the tours disrupting his communing with nature and being one with God. She'd told him that this was a big area and to commune elsewhere. She'd even been somewhat friendly when doing it. She couldn't explain it, but this didn't seem like something he would do.

She waited several more minutes before moving toward the fire, deciding a little light wouldn't hurt. Once the fire was going, she looked around the camp again; it was clean, and there was nothing to attract a bear, excluding whatever Rad had in her tent.

She hated to do it but felt that she needed to wake the other guides as something was not right, and her gut told her that they needed to be prepared.

Chapter Four

Darrell Rowberson was a man of God, and he loved the solace of the mountains, but he loathed the woman who brought her ATV tours every week. The noise from their camp drifted across the valley and infuriated him. He had come here for peace, and how dare she and her clients ruin it for him?

He knew he was close to snapping, and that is why he had left the city; no one knew who he was or where he had gone. He'd dishonored the Lord when he'd broken his vow of celibacy. The fact that he had done it with an underage prostitute was simply the icing on the cake.

His was not Catholic, but honoring the Lord through celibacy was how he chose to live his life; it was what he preached to the congregation.

The truth was Darrell enjoyed the bountiful pleasures of youth and had "mentored" many young boys through the years. He failed to see the harm in two people pleasuring each other as long as it was consensual.

He would still be leading his congregation had it not been for one misstep with the whore. Darrell knew it was a sin, but he preferred boys to girls; there was no chance of breaking his celibacy vow with the boys, he reasoned. After years of experimenting with the nubile boys did his carnal desire finally break free in him, and it was only then that he sought the company of a woman. Touching was one thing, but to fornicate with the boys was a sin punishable by death. Had the Lord not rained sulfur down upon Sodom and Gomorrah?

When he'd been arrested, the people had turned against him. Before he was even released from incarceration, word of his sin had quickly spread. Only hours had passed, but Darrell found himself homeless and without a place to lay his head, the church owned the home in which he'd lived. The people who had once called him friend had taken it upon themselves to rid his private space of all possessions. He'd thought himself lucky that they hadn't burned his worldly goods, even more thankful they had not found his little treasures. Treasures he kept to remind him of each young boy who he'd mentored. He cringed to think of what would have happened then. It was bad enough that, in one night, life as he knew it imploded, but had his true secret been revealed, Darrell knew that what little slice of life he had left, would be spent in hell on earth. Prison.

He'd packed his old Ford truck and headed across Montana thinking that he would simply settle in a small town and continue to preach the gospel. He soon found that it was not that easy; people feared and questioned religion, and within days his sin had been revealed, again he found himself shunned. Having no money and no desire to find other work, he decided to go to ground, certain that the Lord would forgive him his sin and absolve him of this heavy burden he carried. He chose a spot on the map and drove until there were no more roads; there he'd set up camp and went about his prayers, hoping the Lord would show him the way to salvation.

That had been two months ago; these wilderness tours were already in full swing. Darrell had approached the woman asking her to relinquish the mountain to him so that he could find peace and salvation from God. He'd explained that she was disrupting the Lord's will. She needn't know that so far he'd received no divine intervention leading him to a glorious path of righteousness.

Darrell had immediately disliked her and believed in his soul that it was the bitch's fault. He'd smelled the loathing and disgust seeping out of her pores when she had in no uncertain terms told him to go to hell and stay away. He remembered her face as if it were just yesterday. Her mouth was twisted into a scowl, her eyes narrowed in contempt for his religious plight. She'd produced official documents from the Forest Service granting her the right to be there and dared ask him what documents he had giving him the right to intrude on her solace.

Darrell felt hatred building in his chest and with what little dignity he could muster, told her that he was a man of God and did not need permission from the government. He had been sent to do the Lord's work, and it was He who wanted him there. Even as the lie slid so easily from his mouth, he could tell she didn't believe a word he'd preached; the set of her shoulders and tick in her jaw clearly expressed her lack of empathy. She'd merely pointed into the distance and told him he'd "better start to stepping" because it was a real bad time of the month, and it had been a helluva long time since she'd shot anything."

He had been horrified that she would speak of such unseemly things in his presence; he could only sputter God's word on the topic, but as she reached for the menacing shotgun at her side, he'd retreated like a whipped puppy. Tail between his legs and nearly soiling himself, Darrell had run from her camp.

Darrell loathed her and tonight he'd intended to sneak over on this first night of her tour. He would act the part of a crazy mountain man. He knew the bitch would not back down, but he hoped to scare the tourists enough that she would be forced to leave.

It was nearly midnight when he'd begun his hike, feeling like it was the Lord's will that guided him. Finally, a sign, he thought.

Darrell remembered a time when he would have been loath to call any woman a bitch, but things changed. People changed, he'd changed, and not for the better. He only wanted to find himself and justified his actions that it was what God would want. He had hiked nearly half way to the woman's camp when a feeling of unease settled over him; he felt watched. Was it finally possible that God was watching over him? But why would he feel uneasy if it was God? He'd spent enough time in the forest to know that what watched him was not a Holy presence.

He didn't believe in hunting and felt that owning a gun would go against his beliefs that all life was precious and to be honored. For the first time since his arrival in the mountains, he wished he'd at least had the forethought to think of his own personal safety. He would just have to keep his faith that whatever danger he faced would simply be God's will.

***

The beast rumbled low in his throat as he watched the man approach. This human was another bother that Kretha wished to be done with. Why did man think they had the right to intrude upon the forest that had belonged to his Clan for centuries?

His Clan had evolved and hidden when first the tree cutters came and hauled away the giant trees that had camouflaged their existence. The Clan had taken to the ground and sought shelter in caves and dark timber yet untouched by the humans. This made foraging for food and drink harder, his hunters often risked being seen so that the Clan had food. This season, the Gods, had not been angry and threw no fire, the forests remained wet and cool. This was one small pleasure in what had become an inhospitable land.

Kretha raised his eyes to the sky where the ancient Gods resided; he knew, however, that they would offer no help. Where had the Gods been when his mother was shot and killed by humans? Her body stolen and put into a Noise Maker never to be seen again, it was the Law that the Leviathans bury their dead and perform a ritual that would ensure the departed made it safely to the heavens. His mother was weak; she'd sacrificed herself believing that Kretha could escape and reunite with their Clan.

He had been a cub when the humans had come in the night; his mother was trapped in the open, and he'd watched her stand there as the human's Pain Sticks filled her body with their fire. She'd had enough time to hide him and command he stay quiet no matter the cost. Kretha had remained hidden in the tree for two suns until hunters from his Clan finally found him. He'd been terrified, starving, and cold, but it was then that he knew he would one day rule his Clan, and all humans would be expelled from the forests. The Old Ones' Law said that a Leviathan must never kill a human; Kretha and his Clan had upheld this Law using other ways to remove the threat. The beast growled again as he thought of his mother allowing herself to be killed; she was the reason he disliked all the females. He would not have taken a mate if not for the urge to sire a son and the importance of keeping the species alive.

The aggressive tactics used by the watchers had always worked before; of course, there were never many humans in this area, and the Clan was able to stay safely hidden. Even the female and other humans with the Noise Makers that came during the hot season didn't bother their existence. Last year when the other Clan had moved in and brought chaos, Kretha had merely moved the Clan deeper into the forest and posted watchers. Others of his kind would be able to smell them and recognize the sign that they diligently hid from the humans, but they remained hidden and safe throughout the ordeal.

Luckily, the turmoil last season hadn't reached his family, and most remained unaware of what happened. Kretha was pleased when the Clan from the west had left, but then they returned when winter's snows melted. Kretha knew the Clan was guided by a giant red Leviathan, and it was he, the Chief, whom he'd watched welcome the humans. This involvement with the humans was what disturbed him the most; it broke the Law, but they stayed far away and kept to themselves. He would not challenge the new Clan, but neither would he welcome any human into his territory.

Kretha watched as the man stopped and looked around; he knew the human felt his eyes boring into his soul. There was nothing more that he desired at this moment than to step out and end the life of the man. He was alone, his watchers and hunters guarding the Clan, and no one would be the wiser. Kretha knew, though, that once he let his rage free, he would not be able to reign himself in.

He would never eat the pathetic humans, the idea sickened him, he was pleased that both of the flesh eaters from the other Clan had fought to their death and would not pose a threat.

Kretha knew that his kind were often spotted by humans, and their existence was not as closely guarded as it once had been, but he'd seen firsthand what happened when the Pain Sticks threw their fireballs into flesh. What if the old man carried one with him? The idea that the man would ever know the great Kretha was about to kill him was laughable. Kretha didn't even know he was going to do it until he felt his massive bulk step from the shadows.

****

Darrell was being watched; he felt it in the marrow of his bones, and he knew not what it was. He'd heard locals talk about a rogue grizzly that killed several people in these woods last summer, but so far he hadn't seen any bears, let alone a killer grizzly. He looked around again, and as the wind shifted, he was assaulted by a powerful odor that was indescribable: it was the smell of death.

Darrell Rowberson began to pray to the Lord; he asked forgiveness of his sins and repentance for the bad thoughts and actions he had been about to do. As surely as he knew he'd been being watched, he also knew that tonight would be his last on this earth. He did not believe in

Hell—only a perfect Heaven—and knew that God would
not forsake him.

****

*Kretha stepped into the moonlight and watched as
the old man gaped at him. The human didn't even try to
run, which he was surprised to find very disappointing; it
might have been pleasurable to give chase. Instead the man
fell to his knees, raised his puny arms, and gazed toward
the heavens.*

*As if his God could save him now, Kretha felt a
moment of unease as the human began to speak. He knew
not what he said, nor did he care. He advanced upon the
man, still unsure of how he would kill him, only positive
that he was indeed going to kill him. As he neared the
human, his immense size blocked the moonlight; he
delighted in the terror that filled the human's eyes. The
unease he felt only moments before was forgotten, and the*

giant knew the exact moment when the human knew he was about to die.

****

Darrell had been wrong. Hell did exist, and it stood before him. He knew he saw Bigfoot and for a brief moment thought everything would be fine. Bigfoot didn't exist; this was all just his imagination. But then the beast took two steps, Darrell knew there had never been a killer bear. It was a beast that had hatred blazing in its eyes, its epic size blocked the moonlight, and Darrell could only stare up at it.

The Lord had forsaken him after all; no prayers would save him. As the beast approached, he wished he could shut his eyes and make it all disappear, but it was almost as if he was numb, transfixed by the glare burning into his soul. The beast snarled, and Darrell didn't know if it was a sob or a gasp that left his mouth, his insides trembled, and he felt his arms fall to his sides. Hot tears streaked down his face, and he only briefly registered that snot was dripping into his still-open mouth. He felt his insides spasm and his bowels released; he knew the beast smelled the foul odor because he paused and smelled the air.

When the beast finally stood over him, he thought his heart would explode and prayed to the God he'd once believed in that it would. He knew what was coming and had no desire to be conscious for it.

Darrell Rowberson was a sinner, he'd been a fake his entire life; he knew it, and so did God. He'd lied and cheated honest people out of money, all the while preaching the Commandments to hundreds when he himself had broken them. His Maker was beyond forgiveness.

His heart did explode but not because of a heart attack.

****

Kretha watched the human closely for signs of a Pain Stick but saw none. The human had eliminated himself of his waste, and the smell was repulsive; the Leviathans dug holes and buried their waste. Yet another example of how man was pitiful. His anger flared and he roared his hatred. The man covered his head as if to protect himself, further enraging Kretha. Before he knew it, he had raised his giant foot and was kicking the human through the air.

Satisfaction like he had never known rushed to his brain as he watched the flailing man soar across the clearing. His delight turning to euphoria when, even from this distance, he heard the snapping and crunch of the man's bones breaking. Kretha heard the human's skin tearing as jagged bones ripped through the tender flesh.

For a brief second there was a bloody haze in the air when the body made contact with the tree. And then the man was falling to the ground, where, of course, there was no movement. No life.

Kretha walked toward the dead man, intensely pleased with himself and curious as to what might remain of the human. He would have to clean the mess up and bury the man but not before he got a closer look at his work. There was indeed a mess, but what remained was a pitiful excuse of a human. Of course, they were all pitiful and weak, but this was awe-inspiring to look upon. The man was not only broken, he was pulverized. Where the man's head used to be round, it was now flattened as if the bones inside had turned to liquid.

Bright blood mingled with a grey substance that Kretha had never seen before. They both seeped to the ground to mix with the rest of the remains. White bones dripped with bright red blood where they had torn through the skin. Kretha was not sure where the human's arms and legs were; he presumed they were mingled amidst the pile of gore. Or maybe they were the bones he now stared at. What skin he could see, that was not covered in blood, was already turning a blackish purple. Kretha had seen his own kind be killed before, but what remained was nothing like this.

This reminded him of the afterbirth when his mate had birthed the cubs. Among his Clan, other female members would assist with the birth, but as the Chief and father of the cubs, it was his duty to make sure his offspring were well guarded. None of his Clan would dare rise against him, but it was not unheard of for the male cubs of a Chief to be killed by a rival Clan's hunters.

Kretha had witnessed the birth of both his cubs, and the aftermath. It was almost as repulsive as what was left of the human. He would need to destroy the evidence. Fortunately, he would not need to dig a very big hole. The *blood would dry, but he would be sure to cover it with dirt and other forest debris. It would probably be best to dig the hole near the body; carrying the puddle of human was not possible.*

Kretha completed his task and set out to find water; he was parched. The task of burying the man wasn't really even a task. It took less than ten minutes to dig the hole and be done with it. The energy pulsing through his body was what he loved. He'd known once he started that there would be no stopping.

Chapter Five

Darrell Rowberson was officially dead and buried, yet the young man with hatred and murder burning within his soul had diligently dogged his every move across the state. He couldn't know that his prey had already fallen victim to something far more sinister than Cody's own wrath.

Cody Ronald Lee never considered himself a victim, nor would he ever admit why he hunted the preacher. He knew exactly how that would end. What Cody would admit to was a burning desire to see the old bastard suffer. He needed to see the fear in Darrell Rowberson's eyes as he came face to face with him after all these years.

Rowberson was the destroyer of his childhood and responsible for the many beatings his mother inflicted. The man of God, as he liked to call himself, was the reason he had moved from one worthless foster home to another after the system stepped in.

He moved every couple months for one reason or another. The "forever families," as they liked to call themselves, couldn't handle his emotional outbursts. He was afraid of the dark, afraid of men, and was just "simply too much to handle." Cody finally ending up in a shitty group home in Helena. He'd aged out of the system, but that same system would never leave him.

Cody was born in Three Forks, Montana, but raised in so many different towns that he'd forgotten them all. The families he'd been placed with knew his story, and somehow it always seemed to get around that he was the poor molested boy. Teachers looked at him with pity, and the neighbors never wanted him to play with their kids. He wouldn't have anyway.

It was the kids that were the hardest on him. Once they knew Cody's secret, a Bible would invariably show up in his locker, and notes would be left in his desk asking him if he had gone to church lately.

One of the things that bothered him the most was when a group of girls who knew he was from Three Forks would ask if he'd enjoyed being "forked" or maybe he was a spooner instead. Cody was never able to move past what had happened, and knew he would eventually get even, but what pissed him off the most was four years of high school saddled with the moniker Spooner. It might have been an amusing nickname had it not been a constant reminder of his past.

Cody had been eight years old when the perverted preacher began touching him, and in his innocence, he'd told his mother. She'd been so taken with Rowberson and his gospel that she wouldn't believe little Cody's horrific lies. That is what she had called them, horrific lies. Darrell

Rowberson was the man behind his earliest and worst memories; he was also the catalyst that changed his life and set it on a path of juvenile destruction.

His mother had beaten him and sent him to his room for slandering a good and Godly man. Cody had hoped that he would be forbidden to attend church, but instead his mother drug him to the parish and forced him to look into the eyes of the monster that had violated his trust. His sweet mama that everyone loved then forced Cody to tell Rowberson the slanderous things he had said against him.

As Cody glared at the man responsible for his physical pain, he had stood as tall as any eight-year-old boy could and boldly repeated, word for word, what the man had in fact done to him. Rowberson had acted horrified and shocked and promised his mother that there were no hard feelings; he simply asked that he be allowed to "help Cody find peace and seek the Lord's forgiveness." Of course, she agreed and left him standing there alone with a monster.

That was twelve years and a lifetime ago. It was 2:00 a.m., and Cody had driven nonstop from the North Dakota oil rig where he'd busted his ass in the filth and heat to save enough money to hire a private detective. The detective had called three days ago with Rowberson's location. He was flush with cash and walked off the rig with no notice and no forwarding address. Cody doubted he would need his last paycheck anyway.

After a quick stop in Kalispell to buy a few supplies, he'd pulled through the McDonald's at the edge of town and bought a bag of dollar burgers. He thought it was a testament to his life that what would most likely be his last meal was a greasy piece of meat that was of questionable content. The fact that it cost a buck wasn't lost on him either.

Cody didn't look back as the lights of town faded. He drove into the dark, depending on his GPS to lead him to McKillop Road, seventy miles west of Kalispell. From there he would take a left and head into the mountains following a hand-drawn map to Forest Service road number 17255. The bastard thought he could hide from civilization, but if you had the will and enough money, anyone could be found. Cody didn't know exactly where Rowberson's camp was, but he'd find it and put his torment to rest once and for all.

Chapter Six

Kate had awoken Blake, and together they watched the camp through the night. She still felt uneasy, and sometime around 1:00 a.m. they had heard a chilling roar.

She couldn't imagine what it was but was thankful it was off in the distance.

Blake was silent through much of the night, sensing Kate's mood. Kate liked him; he was a good man. She knew he liked her more than she may have appreciated, but over the years they had just fallen into a routine and it was better they just remain friends. Even though they saw each other all the time, she just had never been inclined to take the next step with him. He'd never pushed, and she appreciated that. Maybe someday their worlds would align, but if truth be told, she still carried a torch for her ex.

She hated going down memory lane, but she still loved Joe. He was just a dumbass that thought he could tell her what to do. No one told Kate what she could and couldn't do—at least not without an explanation—and last summer Joe had gone ballistic when she was going to continue to guide in this area.

He'd never been a fan of her job, but after his nephew went missing and the grizzly had killed so many people, he'd just flipped. Things had gotten ugly, and they began to fight all day every day, so Kate walked away. They'd had no contact since this past spring when she'd attended his nephew Cole's wedding. He barely looked at her, and the reception was less than welcoming.

She'd left right after the wedding and had not seen or heard from him since. She figured the whole thing with Joe was also part of her needing a break and having a pissy attitude.

She was friends with Cole and his wife Mari; in fact, Mari was manning the fire tower again this summer, they saw each other often and were in radio contact almost daily. It was hard being a woman out here, and both Kate and Mari enjoyed each other's company. It was eerily strange that they both came from outdoorsy families and they'd both lost their moms. They joked all the time about their dads and brothers, and Kate knew that even though she was now married, Mari was just as close to her family as she was with hers. Kate suspected that Cole took the Foresters job up there just so he could keep Mari out of trouble. Mari was a free spirit, but if there was trouble, she found it. It was just Kate's dumb luck that she'd been with her on a couple occasions when they'd found trouble. But it was all in good fun.

Cole and Mari had definitely formed a solid bond; they shared something very deep, and Kate had no idea what it was, but whatever it was, they kept it private. If she was honest, she was secretly envious of what they had. All of the Roberts' were good people, and that included Joe.

She missed him but couldn't turn her back on her family and her business. Cole respected Kate, and she knew he kept his comments about his uncle to a minimum so not to rub salt in old wounds. He would often show up here to check on her and the clients, and she wondered if he did it because they were friends or if Joe had asked him to. She figured that was too much to hope for.

Kate added more wood to the fire and again looked to the woods; all was silent. That was what bothered her, though; the mountains were full of life, and the critters had no problems communicating.

Mari had pulled her aside at the beginning of the season and told her to please be careful. She had been vague with her warning, and Kate just thought it was because the grizzly that killed the people last summer was never caught. She hadn't really thought much about Mari's warning until just now and wondered if it had anything to do with Joe freaking out. She just wanted to be done; this season sucked. Kate hoped that her dad and Jace were enjoying their last trips more than she was hers. She'd check in with them tomorrow, but tonight she had clients to look out for.

The headache that plagued her all day had increased to a throbbing roar. The pain and lack of sleep was making her feel edgy and disjointed. Kate didn't like either.

Dawn was approaching, so she might as well start getting things ready for the day. Usually one of the campers assisted with the cooking, but since she was up, she may as well get to it. She looked around for Blake and found him staring off into the night. She called to him quietly and was shocked when he didn't turn toward her; instead, he held up his hand and shook his head. This was the universal symbol for "not now" and "shut the hell up."

Careful of where she stepped, she silently moved across the camp to stand beside him. Kate glanced at him and again was slightly taken aback to see the look on his face. It was cold and unflinching as he continued to watch the woods. Even with dawn approaching, it was still too dark to see inside the timber, so she just stood silently and watched. A twig snapped, the hair on the back of her neck stood up, and her eyes darted to where the sound had come from. Less than sixty yards inside the tree line, she'd guess.

Staring intently into the dark forest wasn't doing her head any favors. The ache intensified, as if that was even possible. She thought there was a good chance she might get sick. Regardless she couldn't let her guard down. Something told her to do so now would mean death.

Kate heard the click of the safety on Blake's rifle; she felt him reach down and unsnap the holster that housed his .45 pistol. Kate had never bothered putting the safety back on the shotgun, so she was ready and thankful that she'd put extra shells in her pockets. She wished she'd clipped her own pistol on when she'd left the tent, but it was still tucked inside her backpack.

Kate had no idea what was out there, but she trusted Blake; she wanted to ask if he'd seen anything, but her gut told her to stay quiet. She glanced around and was immediately relieved to see they were in the shadows.

Hopefully, whatever was inside the timber would have as hard a time seeing them as they did it. She knew better, though; whatever animal it was knew where they were. It was simply The Law of The Forest: If a pine needle fell, an eagle would see it, a deer would hear it, and a bear would smell it.

Again they heard the sharp snap of twig, but this time it was farther in the distance, and Kate was certain she could hear footsteps moving away. It was nearly 6:00 a.m., and the sky was beginning to brighten from the east. She knew, though, that if it was a hungry grizzly, daylight would not stop it from approaching camp.

She glanced at the tents—four in total—and memorized where each party slept. Her tent was the closest to the timber, and that was probably why she'd been alerted

hours earlier. Next to her was the young couple, followed

by the family, and lastly the tent Blake and Shit for Brains

shared. After a brief discussion, she and Blake had decided

not to wake him. Chances were he'd be the first one to fuck

up and get eaten by the bear, shoot himself—or worse, one

of them—in the foot.

She was startled out of her thoughts when Blake

said, "It's gone."

"How do you know? What was it?" Her reply was

clipped. They needed to discuss how to handle it and if it

was safe to remain at the camp. She didn't want the

campers to overhear and freak.

"I have no idea what it was, and as for how I know

it's gone, just call it intuition," he said.

"We need to decide if it's safe to stay here or not,

I'd rather make an informed decision. If I drag these people

back to town and have to refund thousands of dollars, my

ass will be grass if we panicked over a black bear. As soon as it is fully light, I'd like for you to put Dipshit on breakfast duty, and you and I will take a little walk. I don't think we will find anything, but maybe we'll get lucky and find tracks." Kate knew she sounded short, but she also knew Blake understood.

She walked back to the fire and stared into its flames; maybe she should have listened to Joe. She wouldn't be miles in the back country with God only knew what stalking the camp, she wouldn't be exhausted, and most importantly, she wouldn't be single and pining away for a man she'd chosen to leave.

Kate had stood watch even though it was now light so Blake could wake up Dipshit. *Hell*, she thought, *better check that at the door or find herself being taken to court over some bullshit harassment charge.* Today was going to be a long day for sure. When she saw Blake returning, she went to her tent and grabbed her backpack. She was

snapping on her pistol when Richard Cranium finally

emerged from his tent. He looked agitated, and when he

spotted Kate, he stomped over to her.

"I am part of this crew, too, you know. I should

have been woken up. I'm your assistant guide, not Blake."

He was all but shouting, and for all her other faults,

that was one thing Kate didn't do and wasn't about to start.

She was preparing to blow but figured she'd get more

enjoyment out of making him squirm and feel like an ass.

"Listen, I am in no fucking mood to put up with

your little-man syndrome. The bottom line is I

am the owner of this outfit, this is my show, and what I say

or choose to do is not only none of your business, but so

help me God if you dare raise your voice to me ever again,

I will cut out your tongue and shove it up your ass. As for

being my "assistant," I think you are confused as to your

job description. You are the new guy, the greenhorn who

forgot the damn gas for Christ's sake. You are the gopher, and if you want to keep your job, then you will do what I say. When you start signing the paychecks, then you can call the shots, but until that time, and I can assure you, hell will freeze over first, you will treat me with respect. Do I make myself clear?"

Kate had thought she could control her temper, but Dipshit Richard Fucktard Cranium had pushed a button. She glared at him as he stood there staring at her, she could hear Blake whistling as he walked off to get the cached food. She didn't really want anyone going on a walkabout until they had a chance to check things out, but she'd be damned if she'd back down. It would show weakness, and little shits like this fed off others' weaknesses.

She'd gone toe to toe with several male clients in the beginning, stood her ground when an idiotic, drunken log truck driver almost ran her over, told the preacher to go to hell, and that was just the start. She'd started and finished a couple bar fights and even punched a Forest

Service official in the face when he'd propositioned her. Of

course, she'd almost lost her license, but the threat of

sexual harassment put that to bed in short order.

The young man was still clearly angry, but knew he

had overstepped his bounds. The bottom line was he'd been

embarrassed to have slept through the entire ordeal, and it

did nothing for his male pride. He knew, though, that Kate

would serve him walking papers for breakfast, and even he

knew when to shut his mouth. Her paychecks always

cleared, and she paid well for the work they did. Yes, it was

better to shut the hell up. "Yeah, umm, so I may have come

on a little strong, Kate. I apologize. I just feel bad that I was

sleeping while you both were up all night. And I know I

screwed up by forgetting the gas. I guess I was just

embarrassed."

Kate continued to look at him, silently impressed

that he'd had the balls to stand there and let her shred him and then apologize. She still didn't like the little piss ant, but narrowed her eyes and nodded in acceptance of his apology. "You're on breakfast this morning. Have one of the campers help you, but make sure every food scrap is burnt and the food wagon is clean. Blake and I are going to check the woods. I want you to have eyes on every camper, especially the kid. If Rad comes out with any makeup or perfume, you had better make sure it's been washed off and her shit is bagged and away from camp." At his immediate scowl of being put on cooking duty Kate bristled. "I need you to have your shit together; we don't know what was here last night, but it's my guess that it wasn't friendly. And just so we're clear, you are most definitely not being punished by having to help with breakfast. You don't know these woods the way Blake and I do, and quite honestly, I don't know you well enough to trust you in the bush. I don't want one word mentioned to the campers. Did you miss anything? Do I need to repeat myself, Richard, because I fucking hate repeating myself?"

Kate knew she was being a hard-ass; how many guides had bitched at her dad and Jace about her? She didn't give a shit; it was her capital that started this business, and she was in charge of making sure the bills got paid. No one else needed to know, and she was always careful that her dad and Jace were included and that they were all equals. But there just came a point when enough was enough. She'd ended a five-year relationship to keep this ball rolling, damn it.

"I got it, Kate. Umm, just so I can keep it on the down low with the campers, how do you recommend I approach that Rad woman? I don't wanna cause you any trouble. I'd probably tell her to go wash the stinking shit off, but I know that would just get me in trouble. And when they want to know why, what do I say?"

He looked like a lost little boy who was in way over his head. In all reality, he was young, and for all she knew, they were all in over their heads. Her gut told her that the season was not going to end smoothly.

"If she has it on, remind her of the rules and the contract that she signed. If she gives you shit, explain that her foofoo juice will endanger everyone, but point out her own daughter. Keep it cool and act like you're simply doing your job. If she refuses, then radio me. I will be more than happy to point out the rules and refund policy. Consider this your free pass. I expect you to handle it, though. You have to be able to handle the clients. They will test you at every turn, but you can get your point across I'm sure." He looked a little better, and she watched him pull himself together. "And, Richard," she paused so she knew she had his full attention. "Keep your gun near you at all times, and absolutely no one leaves this camp; I don't care if they are shitting their pants. They can go behind the tents and we'll deal with it later. I am hoping to be back before they even wake up."

"Understood, Kate." He nodded his head at her much like she had just done to him. She showed no reaction and offered no response as she picked up the shotgun and her backpack. She had shit to do and standing here wasn't getting it done.

Chapter Seven

Still energized after killing the old man, Kretha decided to check the group of humans led by the female; he had checked earlier, and nothing was any different than what it usually was when she was here. He'd intended to return with one of his hunters and scare them but had gotten sidetracked when he smelled the scent of the man.

The fire that the humans seemed to like had been embers when he was here earlier, but now it was ablaze. Kretha immediately positioned himself in the shadows and was surprised to see the female and the male that was always with her awake. They watched the darkness as if they knew he was here, and they had Pain Sticks! Kretha was immediately angry. They could not know of his presence; it was impossible. The humans acted as if they expected him. The male stared directly at him, but Kretha knew he was hidden. Had one of his hunters come in search of him and alerted the humans?

His anger was consuming him, and in his frustration, he was careless. The branch he'd stepped on broke into tiny pieces; the noise was loud and sharp in the silence of the night. He immediately stopped and looked to the humans; the female had joined the male, and together they glared in his direction.

He'd given away his position! The humans didn't scare him as much as their Pain Sticks did. They could throw the fireballs at him, and he would be defenseless! He had allowed himself to be compromised.

Kretha barely breathed as he silently watched the humans. They had not acted aggressively even though he knew they had heard the branch break. Both humans stood in the shadows, silent and watchful, waiting. He would have to wait them out and hope that the rising sun would not illuminate his hiding spot.

Kretha waited, and while he did, his gaze fell upon the female. He had seen her many times over the years and knew her scent well. She had surprised him on many

occasions. He couldn't understand why she kept returning.

There were always new humans with her, and he wondered

what she did with them, why she brought them here? The

big male was always with her, but his presence did not

bother Kretha.

The female had distracted him on several

occasions; he had heard her laugh for the first time years

ago, and even though he disliked all females and loathed

humans, the sound she emitted was intriguing. He had

allowed her to keep returning and made the watchers and

hunters stand down and allow it to be. Often Kretha found

himself on guard duty just so he could watch the female.

Even as the forest's apex predator, Kretha had no idea

why, when his hatred for females was so great, he enjoyed

the yellow-haired human so much. Her Pain Stick scared

him, but she never seemed aggressive, and more often than

not, the sound of her human laughter brought him happiness.

It was only the past few moons that she had begun to scare him. Now the fear had turned to anger, and Kretha had broken the Old Ones' Law. He'd killed because of her.

Kretha could have easily killed the female several times over the years, but there had never been the desire. Even now, having killed for the first time, he had no desire to end her life. The rest did not matter to him—alive or dead—he just wanted them gone. Why had she changed?

Tonight there was no laughter as her gaze penetrated the forest. Kretha felt the power she emitted; she stood unflinching, her gaze never shifting from his position. He knew in that moment that she was a problem.

Kretha knew that if she sensed a threat, she would react the same as what he would: she would fight or die trying. He weighed over eight hundred pounds and could easily destroy her, but he had never seen her without her

Pain Stick. He would never admit it, but he suspected this female was his equal. That thought sparked anger, and he felt himself tightening, ready to charge.

He stopped himself as the winds shifted, and he smelled her; he didn't know if she could feel his presence, but for several heartbeats their eyes were locked. The anger retreated as he cautiously backed up, being as silent as possible. When he felt safe, he turned and walked away, not understanding what had happened.

The mighty Kretha felt certain the female had entered his mind and issued a warning. The iron-fisted Chief of his Clan had just allowed a human female to rule his mind. Kretha did not understand the human's language, but he knew without a doubt what her warning had been. It was as if she'd walked up to him and spoken his language, "Come any closer and you will die this day." He believed her.

Chapter Eight

Kate was exhausted, and the day was just beginning. She couldn't shake the feeling that she wasn't finished with whatever was hiding in the trees. As she'd stood next to Blake, she knew that whatever lurked in the shadows was staring at her; she felt it to her core. Kate had readied herself for an attack and silently vowed that whatever watched her, would die if it came one step closer.

The exchange with Richard had fueled the urge to strike, and even now as she entered the shadowy forest, she was ready.

She and Blake paused, without speaking, right inside the shadows to allow their eyes to adjust. The morning sun had not yet lit the forest completely. She agreed with Blake that whatever had been here was gone, but she didn't want to miss a clue in the poor light. As Blake went to move, she gently laid her hand on his arm.

He stopped and glanced at her, but she just shrugged. They would wait.

The sounds of the forest had returned, offering a small amount of comfort to Kate, but Joe and Mari's warnings echoed through her mind. She flashed back to the arguments with Joe, and it was almost as if she was seeing what he saw! Kate saw Adam Brody's lifeless body being consumed by a beast that took her breath away. She saw Cole hiding and then he and Mari running from something that meant to kill them. She saw the fire raging all around them, and the bodies piled up before her eyes.

Her breath caught and she glanced at Blake to see if he was watching her. He stared into the shadows unaware of what had just happened.

Kate's headache exploded behind her eyes as she watched Dylan Thomas shoot one of the epic beasts, but it didn't end; two of the giants exploded into one. The one Dylan had shot had killed the savage and was returning a dead body to the group of searchers; it was there that the beast collapsed and died. Above all else she saw Joe, her Joe, standing in the background watching everything.

Holy shit, it couldn't be! But Joe was an avid outdoorsman, and what happened last year changed him; he would never freak out over a bear, even a killer grizzly. Damn him to hell, he'd lied to her! It was never a fucking grizzly. Why he hadn't just told her blew her mind; he'd kept it from her knowing that it or they had killed several people for God's sake! Led her to believe it was a bear! A bear—even a pissed off grizzly—was manageable, but this, this was not acceptable!

Christ, she'd wondered over the years if the stories were true and secretly believed they were here, but she never thought they were dangerous. There was no doubt in her mind that what was here last night was no longer unknown. Blake startled her out of her whirling thoughts. "You ready?" he asked.

Holy mother of all hell, no she wasn't ready! She couldn't say a thing; not even Blake would buy what she knew to be living here. Bigfoot? The secret that Mari and Cole shared made perfect sense now, but why the hell would they come back?

She looked at Blake and shook her head. "No, we absolutely do not go into the forest, and no one else does either. I need to do something first." She was backing out of the timber all the while conscious that her friend watched her with an astonished look on his face.

"Kate? What just happened? Are you okay?"

"I'm fine. Stay out of the forest and keep everyone close. You need to trust me, please." She looked at him and silently pleaded with him to follow her and not ask questions. He nodded and followed her back to camp. No one was up yet, and she caught the surprised look on Richard's face when they returned so quickly. It struck her as odd that she'd called him Richard all morning. Kate didn't even know if that was his name and didn't have time to stop and ask.

She rushed past, pulling the satellite phone from her pack as she went. God damn Joe Roberts! She was so livid she'd forgotten to breath and was close to blacking out when she got to the cook trailer. They kept the cooking facilities away from the main camp, and Kate was going to need privacy for this call.

Christ, why wouldn't Mari have told her? Cole was her friend! Her fingers trembled as she dialed Joe's number from memory. He had better answer the phone; he'd know the number, but she had no idea if he would pick up. If he didn't, and she made it out of here alive, she'd castrate him.

It didn't matter that she loved his lying ass, he could have told her! She wouldn't have ever said anything, but instead he'd tried to bully her, and in the end, he still lost the fight and allowed her to walk into a fucking death trap.

She was getting ready to give up when he picked up on the fifth ring.

His answer was an angry, "What do you want, Kate?"

"You lying son of a bitch! I swear to God if fucking Bigfoot doesn't kill me first, when I get out of here, you're going to wish he'd got you last summer!"

"Jesus, Kate! Fuck! Where are you? Please tell me you're not up there!" His voice was shaking in panic. She could hear him rustling around, and in that moment, knew that it was true.

"How could you, Joe?" Kate's voice was small and shattered as she silently hung up the phone; she heard him calling her name but didn't care. They needed help, and she couldn't depend on Joe to give it. Her fingers trembled as she dialed Mari's phone.

She answered on the first ring. "Hey, Kate, I thought you were guiding this week."

"Mari," Kate's voice was shaking, "I'm at Grizzly Lake." She didn't have the breath to go on, her mouth was dry, and she had to sit down. Mari must have heard the panic in her voice because all Kate heard was, "Oh God, Kate, no! Kate? Kate, please answer me! KATE!"

Mari sounded like she was in a tunnel and so far away. Kate knew that she needed to breathe and calm down. She'd been coming here for years and hadn't been bothered. Last night was a warning, that's all. A warning she would heed. Kate disconnected the call and pocketed the phone. She had no idea what to tell her clients, but first she needed to pull her shit together. She was a leader, the leader of this shit storm; she would never depend on help from anyone but herself. She let herself breathe, and her vision cleared. The hard-ass bitch that no one liked was coming back; she stiffened her spine and decided the only thing to do was get her clients out alive.

The phone began ringing almost immediately, and she glanced at the caller ID. *Joe, fine fucking time to want to talk about this shit*, Kate thought as she hit the disconnect button, silencing the phone.

She needed to think. Joe was adamant about the danger of this area, but Mari and Cole were less than five miles away. They spent all their spare time here. None of it made sense. She'd heard the panic in Mari's voice, but why would she be alone up there if she was scared and knew there was imminent danger? For a brief second, she thought about calling her dad and Jace but couldn't bring herself to involve them.

Okay, so she'd tell everyone it was an emergency and throw them on the machines if she had to. Hell, Kate figured she'd push them the ten miles if she had to, but they had to get out of here and do it before dark. A quick glance at her watch told her it was already past 9:00 a.m. Crap, the time had gotten away from her; how long had she been sitting here? Kate jumped to her feet and sprinted back to camp.

She was met with more than one questioning look but ignored them, seeking out Blake. He stood next to Richard, and the minute he spotted her, he ran toward her. His face was pale, and Kate immediately knew something was wrong.

"We have to go now," Kate said.

"Wait, what? Shit! Kate, Rad got pissed and took off when she was told she couldn't wear her perfume. I've looked for her and called, but I can't find her." Kate heard Blake's words, but she was in the tunnel again. Oh God, this wasn't happening! He'd pulled her aside and was speaking in a whisper. Kate's eyes snapped to his the moment she realized the implication of what this meant.

"Blake, listen to me. Please don't interrupt; you need to hear what I have to say. I saw something this morning, I felt it, and if you never believe a word I ever say again, believe me now." He nodded for her to continue.

"Remember me telling you why Joe and I broke up? Remember the grizzly that killed all those people last year when Cole went missing? It wasn't a grizzly. Christ, it wasn't a bear at all. I don't know exactly what happened this morning, but I saw it. I called Joe, and I also called Mari. We're not safe, Blake."

"Kate, what are you saying exactly?" Blake's voice was surprisingly calm. Kate looked at him closely; he looked almost casual. He knew! Did every damned person know but her?

"You know, don't you? Why wouldn't you say anything if you knew we were in danger? I trusted you, Blake; I trusted all of you, and not one of you shared what was here. You all let me drag innocent people up here knowing what had killed those people." She took a step away from him knowing that her face showed the hurt and terror she was feeling. "And now you tell me one of my clients is missing? You're all bastards, and you can consider yourself fucking fired."

"Kate, please just hear me out. I didn't know until this morning! I'd heard stories is all; this morning when I heard the howl, I began to suspect they were true. I promise you I wasn't one hundred percent sure until you just told me. I would never endanger anyone, Kate, let alone you. You have to know that!"

Kate looked at him, and knew he told the truth. She was immediately sorry for yelling at him, but they were in serious trouble; Kate knew it like she knew her last name.

"What are we going to do?" she whispered.

Chapter Nine

Joe Roberts had experienced fear before but nothing like this. It had been a year since he'd gone into the mountains; he knew their secrets, and he'd never wanted to experience them again. He thought of Cole and Mari and knew they had their own secrets, but this was bad. He'd done everything but tie Kate up to keep her out of those mountains, and in the end, he'd pushed her away and right into the danger.

If it was the last thing he ever did, he would save her. The terror in her voice would haunt him for the rest of his life. His Katie didn't panic—she was tough as nails— and if she'd reached out to him, then she'd been scared. What the hell had happened? He was there when the killer had been taken out by one of his own kind, and he knew for certain the others in the area were peaceful.

Oh God, Grizzly Lake was less than two miles from Sylvia. He immediately thought of Silas Baldwin and the story he'd told that afternoon on the mountain after they'd found the blood-soaked clearing where Willy Norman had been killed. He'd tried calling her back, but the call was terminated; she was shutting the ringer off.

He called his nephew next, and Cole was on his way to the fire tower. Kate had apparently called Mari and then hung up. Joe knew that Cole and Mari had the power to help her. Joe had two phone calls to make, and he made them as he gathered his gear. The first was to his brother, Jack. Cole had called Jack and he was already on his way, but it wasn't his brother he wanted. It wasn't a matter of want, it was desperate need. He needed Dylan Thomas.

****

Mari was terrified. Where was Cole? She'd called him and knew he was coming. She'd abandoned her post at the fire tower and did the only two things she could. She called her brother, Dylan, and yelled for Red. He was never far away, and she was terrified that she would be putting his life in danger. But she needed to save her best friend. Red had watchers monitoring the Clan from across the mountains. Red wouldn't have done it if he hadn't been worried.

Mari had tried to warn Kate earlier this summer, but Kate had been guiding into that lake for years and even ventured up to Sylvia and never mentioned a thing. Mari prayed that it was okay; if the other Clan had meant to harm her, wouldn't they have done it years ago?

Red and two of his hunters emerged from the trees below the lookout, and upon seeing Mari; the giant red beast broke into a sprint.

****

Khryl was playing with Nyah when he'd heard his Merr-ee yelling for him. He placed his cub in the arms of his mate, Senna, and whistled for Rooba and Cro. Khryl knew that it was always a danger to expose themselves during daylight hours, but Merr-ee wouldn't have yelled

for him if it was not important.

Khryl stopped his hunters just inside the timber and

waited. When he spotted Merr-ee running toward him, he

knew it was safe. She would never expose him or the Clan if

there was danger near. He scented the air, as did his

hunters, and Merr-ee's was the only smell in the air. He

raced toward her, knowing that Rooba and Cro would be at

his side. As the beasts neared the female who they all

considered part of their Clan, Khryl was immediately

angry. Merr-ee was scared. He'd seen that look on her face

before and knew there could only be one reason for her

fear.

He got to her before the others, and she used his

language to tell him what was happening. Khryl knew of

her friend and had seen her several times when she came to

see Merr-ee; he knew she was important to her and Kooal.

Khryl knew her scent and had placed watchers across the mountain earlier in the season to protect her. The Clan had not bothered the female, so he had called the watchers home. It was nearing time to gather food for the winter, and his Clan was still recovering from the loss of two of their best hunters. He would not think of Thor and Churel now. He reassured Merr-ee that he would see to her friend and sent Rooba and Cro on their way.

Khryl knew his warriors were larger and more than able to defend themselves against the other Clan, but he had one fear. The Chief gazed at Merr-ee and in her language asked, "Where's Dylan?" He knew his friend would not harm Rooba and Cro; Khryl knew that the sibling to Merr-ee would protect his Clan and considered him one of his Clan's warriors.

Khryl also knew the human male could be dangerous and carried a large Pain Stick. He expressed to Merr-ee that her sibling not harm any of the Clan's innocents. Rogues were not tolerated, and the brother would do whatever it took to eliminate them. He did not wish to start warring with a Clan if their innocents were harmed.

His Merr-ee nodded and said it was taken care of; Dylan would be there but knew the rules. He hugged his human and turned her back toward her shelter. She resisted at first, but the sound of an approaching Noise Maker distracted her. Khryl knew it was Kooal; his senses were far superior to any other animal and he had known it was Kooal approaching by his scent.

His other human jumped out of his Noise Maker, and Khryl waited while Merr-ee explained what was happening. When Merr-ee's mate looked at him, the Chief knew he intended to go into the mountains. Khryl and his warriors could sprint the distance in a matter of minutes, but Kooal would never leave Merr-ee's friend.

****

Mari watched from the tower as her husband and her Bigfoot went in opposite directions. This could not be happening again, and Kate was not answering; she had no idea how bad things even were. Maybe Kate had just spotted one and freaked out. She should have told her friend. She'd never forgive herself if Kate got hurt.

****

Dylan Thomas was fishing when his phone rang. He didn't need to see the caller ID to know it was Mari. He'd given her a special ring tone and was never too far when she was manning the fire tower. He'd been excited when Mari and Cole had brought him in on their secret and even honored when the Clan had welcomed him. His wife wasn't thrilled by his new job of Sasquatch Security, but she'd accepted it and was even considering visiting for herself.

His dad had bought a brand new fifth wheel, and for the most part Dylan, his wife, son, and dad stayed the summer on the river. Never too far from the action—or the trouble that was Mari, depending on the day and what she was doing. When his business called for it, Dylan would make arrangements with Cole to cover his absence, and together they kept Red and his Clan safe.

When Mari explained what was happening, Dylan was already on the move. His gear and guns never left the truck. He didn't think there was time to stop by camp, so he radioed his dad, and even though Matt was ready to go, Dylan told him that Kate was at least ten miles in the back country, and he should wait for Cole's dad, Jack, to get there, and then hopefully Dylan would have an OP's report.

Dylan knew that there would be no stopping Joe Roberts from getting to Kate and mentally checked his supplies. Fortunately, his ATV was always fueled and loaded in the truck, and Dylan's wife made sure there was plenty of food. Cole would meet him at the trailhead, and together they would assess the situation and proceed. Mari told him that Red, Rooba, and Cro were dispatched as well.

It was going to be a full house, and he was not to kill anything that had not gone rogue. Yup, he got it: no starting a Bigfoot war.

He was ready; it had been a year since the other chaos had played itself out, and Dylan still felt bad for shooting that big bastard, Thor. In all honesty, he didn't really want to have to shoot any Bigfoot, but shit happened, and this whole Bigfoot thing put an entirely new meaning on guerilla warfare. The giant hair balls always seemed to have a bad seed, and it was those bad seeds that Dylan had no problem exterminating.

He didn't like the idea of riding into hostile territory without his gun in his hand. He'd have liked to have a little more backup than just Cole, but it didn't matter; he was more than capable.

His phone rang again, and it was a number he didn't know; he hoped it wasn't business because he didn't have time for any bullshit. Last year the entire family had sprung for satellite phones, and sometimes the damn thing rang at less than opportune times.

"Hello." His answer was gruff and no nonsense.

"Dylan, its Joe Roberts. There's a problem, and I need you; name your price."

"Hey, Joe, nice of you to keep in touch, man. How's shit? Oh yeah, your girlfriend placed a call to my sister, and it didn't sound like things were good. How's about you meet your nephew and me at the trailhead, and don't fuck around; I want to see some big guns." Dylan snickered as he punched the disconnect button. He wasn't going to make the man beg, nor would he accept money, but the fuck shit should have told Kate what she was in for. In fact, they all owed it to her, and not one of them had spoken up. In Dylan's eyes, they were all a bunch of assholes, and Joe was the biggest. It was his fiancée that he'd put in danger. Kate wouldn't have blinked an eye or said shit to anyone; she would have simply rearranged her guided trips. This secrecy thing was bullshit when it was putting lives in danger, and when this gig was up; Dylan was going to explain how shit was going to happen.

In the meantime, he'd caught up to the dust cloud in front of him and wasn't surprised to see Cole Roberts tearing up the road in his official work truck. He was a good man; his sister got lucky. Someone actually willing to put up with her shit, Cole deserved a metal or sainthood. Something—because Dylan knew Mari could be a ton of trouble. Oh well, it was Mari. What could he do?

****

Cole had seen Dylan pull up behind him and put on a little more speed. He felt better knowing that Dylan was going in with him. He knew Red and his hunters would probably have the problem taken care of, but he knew Joe would be getting there about the same time, and no offense to his uncle, but Cole had little faith in Joe's ability to keep his shit together when it came to Kate. No, even though

Dylan was a crazy son of a bitch, he was badass and had the balls and equipment to pull it off. He reached for the radio—might as well start making a plan with Montana's version of a mercenary.

Chapter Ten

Rad was still missing. Kate had to admit it was time to be honest and let these people know what the hell was happening. Blake had pulled Richard aside and explained the situation, and to Kate's surprise, he nodded and remained calm. He deferred to her for instructions, and so far he had followed them to the letter. Kate supposed that it was time to break the news.

"Hey guys. . .and gals, we need to talk. I think everyone is aware of the tension, and of course, we are all worried about Rad. It's my hope that she is just chilling in the woods trying to make us sweat a little. Here is the thing, the woods are not safe, which means she is not safe, but neither are we. The guides and I all carry weapons and have efficient ammo, but we need to make a plan; the bottom line is we need to reach the trailhead before dark."

Kate was prepared for a fight about the possibility of leaving the woman behind, but everyone just gaped at her.

"Kate, what kind of trouble are we dealing with? I mean, I am not trying to be an asshole, but I've spent eight years in the military; I might not be familiar with these woods, but I know my way around a gun," said Ben. He sat next to Mimi, and the woman looked up and said, "I'm a hunter; I know the woods—just not these woods—and I am also proficient with any gun you have. Ben and I are long distance runners and can climb any rock, cliff, or mountain. How can we help?" Kate was astonished, but just sat quietly for a second. She had no idea how to tell them what was out here.

"Okay, here's what happened." She started from the beginning when she thought someone was still awake and ended with what she saw. She left out the part about her friends keeping such an important secret from her. She looked at the faces around her and found herself drawn to the little girl. Kate could not remember how old she was, but she was tiny and her eyes were red-rimmed from crying. Any mother that would do this to a child and make her worry deserved to be left behind. She glanced at Jeff, and was not surprised in the least to see a blank expression on his face. He would be no help, and chances were he wouldn't even be able to protect his daughter.

Shaking her head in disgust, Kate couldn't help but think, both Jeff and Rad were worthless pieces of shit. Unfortunate as it may be for the girl, it might be best for humanity in general if the beast culled the herd.

"Okay, so we'll search one hour for Rad; after that I am calling in search and rescue, and if she's hiding out being a shit, they're going to be none too pleased. I suggest you all pack your gear and make it quick. Richard, I want you to check every ATV, make sure they are fueled up, and start them. The noise will hopefully deter any predators;

plus, they will be ready to haul ass. Blake, I know you carry an extra pistol in your gear. Would you mind loaning it to Ben? And I will give Mimi my .45. I'd like both of you to maintain the perimeter, keep your backs to camp, watch every shadow, and listen. I'm not gonna lie: I smelled something last night and so be vigilant. I am hoping we'll have some warning. Ben and Mimi, please pack your backpacks with only items that are essential, like extra clothes and water. Wear them and be prepared for the worst. Jeff, you and Marley need to pack, and do not even think about moving from this fire. Jeff, your job is to keep this fire big, do you understand?" He simply nodded, and Kate knew he would not only be unable to look out for his kid, but the pansy-ass fuck probably couldn't keep the fire burning."

Richard, when you're done with the ATVs, could you throw together some food—maybe just sandwiches or anything we can take with us? By the way, outstanding job this morning; you did well and followed my directions. I can see it in your face you feel guilty about Rad running off, but she is an adult and made a choice. Blake and I will search the woods for an hour. Okay, Ben, I trust the camp's security to you. Are you up for it?" She pointedly looked at Mimi and then back at Marley. Mimi caught the look and nodded that she had the child's back. "Anyone have any questions about what their responsibilities are for the next hour?"

Everyone nodded except for Jeff. Kate had more faith in the little girl than she did his dumb ass.

"Kate, I would not have normally said anything, but of course, we read about the grizzly from last year, and since your brochure didn't prohibit it, both of us are armed." This came from Ben as both he and Mimi produced stainless .45's with plenty of ammunition.

"It's completely fine, Ben. Lots of people come armed, and I am glad you are, that leaves both Blake and I our weapons. Now let's get to it; I want to be riding out of this place no later than noon. That will still have us traveling in the dark, and I don't like it."

As they dispersed, Kate saw Marley head toward the tent to complete her assignment, but the idiot, Jeff, just sat there. So Kate went up to him and knelt down and stared him in the eye. He just glared back at her. In a whisper she said, "Listen up, shithead, your wife has really screwed us, now you're being a jackass. Your own daughter is packing her bag; I will not allow you to sit here with your thumbs up your ass. I'll give you one minute to get your ass moving, or you will be staying behind."

"Fuck you. You think you're a badass, don't you? Well, when we get out of here, I'm going to sue you for every penny you have. You've put us all in danger, and now my wife is gone."

"Well, Jeff, you can do whatever the hell you want, but let's get one thing straight between us, and I don't mean your dick. I think you're a colossal prick and a waste of skin. Frankly, you're stealing my oxygen and the oxygen of your little girl. So if you wanna sit here doing nothing, go for it, but when this party leaves, you will not be going with us. This is life and death, shit for brains, do your part. I have no room for your bullshit and extra baggage. As for your dumb ass suing me? Go right ahead, but I am betting you a hundred bucks you won't leave this mountain alive unless you listen. Now your minute is almost up; what's it going to be? You're testing my patience, and I give exactly zero fucks about you."

"God, what is your problem? My wife is missing, and you're being a total bitch."

"Yup, your wife is an idiot that ran off into the wilderness after having a bitch fit because she wasn't allowed to spray shit that would attract wild animals. Until I know differently, I am blaming her for bringing this beast to my camp. Five years I've been coming here and never a problem. One night with your bawl-baby, bitch-titted wife, and we're all in danger."

Kate stood so she had the advantage of height on her side and looked at the loser, "Mark my words: I will leave your sorry ass here, so get moving."

Chapter Eleven

Radka Menke was seriously pissed off. She had an image to uphold, and who were these backwoods shits to tell her she couldn't look her best even stuck way out here in the sticks?

She'd suspected Jeff had been cheating on her, so she demanded that he pay for a new set of boobs in the hope that if she looked better he would drop whatever bimbo he was doing and spend more time at home with her and Marley.

The new boobs hadn't fazed him; losing weight and taking better care of herself didn't get through to him either, so Rad had just quit caring. It wasn't until she had started noticing that other men were staring at her that she decided to play up what she had. She would never cheat on her husband, but she would take whatever attention she could get. It all seemed really stupid now, though, as she sat on a log hopelessly lost and surrounded by nothing but trees and dark shadows. Believe it or not, this trip had been her idea. One last ditch, pathetic attempt to repair what had once been a great marriage to a man that was clueless.

Her family had been so angry when she'd moved to the states to marry Jeff, and even though she didn't love him at the time, it was an escape. When her papa had insisted on her marrying, she had sought out the first handsome man she could find and hung on for dear life.

Jeff had become her ticket to freedom. He'd taken her away from the manual labor of working and living in a tiny village so close to the Siberian border in Russia that for all intents and purposes, may well have been Siberia.

The things she'd had to do as a teenager to bring money and food to her family still made her cringe. When she met Jeff, Radka had never told him of her previous life. Explaining only that her family was dead, and to her, they were. She vowed if she ever had a child, it would never know the life she had. When Marley had been born, it was if she, too, had been reborn. Life had been wonderful until a year ago when Jeff started working more, which eventually turned into him just staying over at the office.

Radka was most likely born in a barn and in the dark, but it hadn't been yesterday; a wife just knew, and what saddened her most was that she sincerely loved him.

She'd wandered a long way from camp, not even realizing it until she glanced at her watch and noticed several hours had gone by. It wasn't hard to get turned around in the woods. She knew that from her childhood, but she was careful and was making her way back toward camp wondering how she was going to save face in front of all those people. She was embarrassed and had several more days stuck up here; it wasn't being in the woods that bothered her.

She had Marley, and her daughter was her world. What bothered her was the look of disgust and contempt on

Jeff's face as she'd challenged the guide. Five days up here with him, would kill her—break her heart and her spirit.

There was nothing she could do about it, though; just find a way to get through it, and when they got home, she would file for a divorce. She loved her husband but would never stand by and watch as he looked at her that way again.

Her papa had looked at her in exactly the same way, and look at where it had gotten her. She'd been put in a whorehouse and her wages sent back to her father. At least now, Jeff never slept with her, but she still felt no less like a whore.

****

Kretha had left the female's camp and began his journey back to the Clan when he'd scented another human in his forest. This instantly put him in a foul temper. He was still angry over the warning he'd felt from the female. It was not like him to walk away from a challenge.

He stood among the shadows and watched as another woman came walking through the trees. This one smelled different than the other, and her tears did nothing to soften the anger within the beast. Females were so weak and pathetic. The human approached, apparently unaware of his presence. He did nothing to camouflage himself, knowing that only her death would satisfy his anger, be the balm to the sting he felt when he thought of the other female's arrogance.

When she was close enough, he let out a snarl.

****

Radka Menke knew exactly what she stared at; the snarl from the beast had gotten her attention. "Yeti," she said out loud. There was no point running from the beast, in her home country it was known to be white. Here in the mountains, she was not surprised to see it darker in color. *Better to camouflage itself*, she thought.

She dropped to her knees and lowered her head. Her grandfather had told her of legends when she was a young girl; he'd said you must always show the beast respect, or it would surely kill you. Rad had always believed her papa's stories and prayed that he was right; if not, she would be seeing him in Heaven soon.

****

Kretha stared in disbelief at the woman. When she had seen him, she had immediately fallen to her knees and lowered her head in a sign of what the Chief believed to be respect. In his Clan, the females were required to do this within his presence. Did this female know of his kind? His immediate rage began to fall away as he studied her for a moment. She did not quake and sob as the man earlier had done. She remained bowed to him. He moved to stand before her and grunted. When she did not respond he clicked his tongue three times and stomped his mighty foot into the earth.

The female slowly raised her eyes to meet his and quickly placed her tiny human hand over where her heart would be. Kretha was awed at her display of respect; never had any female in his Clan shown such regard for her Chief. Kretha reached down and grasped the female by the arm and jerked her to a standing position. Even at her full height, she barely came to half of his.

Kretha had intended to kill her immediately, but as he'd pulled her up, he'd not seen fear; he'd seen the respect that he'd believed her to have. Her startled scream ripped through the morning as he threw her over his shoulder.

****

Seven heads turned at the sound of Rad's scream. Ben, who was walking along the edge of the camp and closest to the woods, immediately, turned to Kate for guidance as did the others.

Kate had about five seconds to take it all in: Mimi launched herself at the little girl, Richard stood as if rooted in stone. Blake was moving toward her, and Jeff Menke was on a full-out, panic-stricken run toward the woods where his wife had just screamed in terror. Kate rushed toward him in an attempt to stop the man, and she saw Blake turn in his direction as well. In the back of her head, she heard Marley crying and the soothing voice of Mimi trying to calm the girl. Ahead she saw Ben struggle with himself on whether or not to turn his back on the woods or try and stop the man.

Another scream tore through the morning, and Kate could not fault the man for holding his position and guarding camp. Both she and Blake were yelling for Jeff to stop, but where only moments before the man had been comatose, he was now on a full-out sprint. He dodged past Ben and into the darkness of the timber screaming his wife's name. Kate heard herself screaming to stop, but her own voice sounded like it was in slow motion.

Just as Blake was about to enter the timber, Kate regained her senses, and everything she knew to be lurking in these woods came back to her.

"Blake, stop!" she screamed. The guide skidded to a stop and turned to look at her. "Don't go in there. Jesus! Do not fucking go in there!"

"Kate, we've gotta do something!" he said.

"Don't you think I know that? But we know what is out there! I won't let you or anyone else here just commit suicide because two ignorant, fucking assholes didn't listen." Kate was angry and staring down Blake. It was her name whispered in the softest of voices that pulled her back to reality.

"Kate? Where are my mom and dad? Are they going to be okay? When are they coming back?" Marley Menke was standing behind her, face tear-stained and red, hand clutched in Mimi's, staring at her. Kate was shocked by her outburst and looked at the little girl and smiled as best she could.

"I don't know what is happening, Marley; I won't lie to you. I really, really need you to stay with Mimi. Let me try to get some help up here, okay?"

The little girl nodded and looked Kate dead in the eye. "I love my mama, Kate." Marley Menke turned into the waiting arms of Mimi.

Chapter Twelve

Jeff Menke had no idea what came over him. He'd heard Radka scream, and all of a sudden, the years of pain he'd put her through hit him. He was on his feet and running. He heard that bitch, Kate, yelling at him to stop, but hadn't it just been her telling him to get off of his ass and do something? So he ran. When Rad had screamed the second time, he knew he would die trying to fix everything he had done.

He knew her history, and in the beginning he had delighted in the fact that he had rescued her from an illicit past.

As the years wore on and the more money he made, he began to think he was more important than what he really was. He soon began paying hookers because somewhere in his warped sense of manhood he thought his money was power, and he wanted to do things to woman that Rad would never let him do to her; things he knew other men had done.

It enraged him. He turned that rage on her and hit her. When she'd gotten pregnant with Marley, she'd made it clear he could do whatever he wanted with whomever he wanted, but he'd better make sure her bank account was well endowed. If he so much as laid a hand on her, she would kill him in a way that would make him wish he'd fallen into one of the wood chippers at work. Jeff had no doubt that she meant every word she'd said.

He may have never physically touched her again, but a day rarely went by that he didn't remind her of where she had come from and who she would be had it not been for him. It took her walking away this morning for him to realize that after all these years, he loved her, and that through it all, she'd never stepped out on him and done him the way he had done her so often.

****

Kretha was annoyed that the woman had betrayed him by screaming! Now he could hear someone pursuing them in through the bushes; had she not known that he was going to keep her? She had shown him her respect. Yes, she was a pathetic human, but Kretha had heard of other Clans stealing women and using them as slaves. Now he would have to deal with what chased them. Kretha hit the female in the head and knocked her unconscious; she had not struggled, but he did not wish to hear her human screams.

He scented the air and knew that he was pursued by one man; it would be easy to handle the situation. He could smell the same scent on the female and suspected that it was her mate that followed. Maybe he would not kill the female's mate but take him, too. Surely humans could be useful for something.

****

Jon Wilbur was a logging truck driver from way back. He'd hauled logs over so many roads that he'd lost count of the miles. Lost count of the trucks he'd owned and lost and the wrecks he'd had. Hell, he was a grungy ole bastard that would cheat his mama outta her last dollar if the old hag had still been alive. He'd screwed enough people in the logging industry that it was a miracle he still got jobs. It was no small surprise that it was these shit jobs which no one else wanted that he was forced to take.

These early morning hauls sucked ass; he had to be up at 2:00 a.m. just to drive way the hell up here. Then he had to load by himself in the dark before the crews arrived and get the first load to the mill in Libby before noon. Just to make a couple hundred bucks a day. He hated being up in these woods all alone in the dark and was always thankful when the truck was loaded, and he was on his way out. He only had the one load up in this shit hole of a valley, and that pissed him off. But he'd made his bed: piss off one too many a mechanic or official, and this was where you went to die.

He was seventy-five years old for Christ's sake and still humping his back just to make a few bucks.

He'd just geared down for the switchback ahead when he'd caught motion out of the corner of his eye. What the hell? Oh hell no! He was laying on the Jake and reaching for his shotgun and door handle all in one motion.

****

Kretha had lain in wait for the human's mate to catch up. The man's throat was in his grasp before he had any idea that his mate was slung over the Chief's other shoulder. The man struggled in vain, but Kretha only squeezed harder, careful not to kill the human. The Chief knew his strength was profound, and he did not want the human dead.

Once the human male was subdued, Kretha ran. He worried that the other humans with their Pain Sticks would soon give chase. In minutes he was a safe distance away from the female, she, who had entered his mind. Kretha knew he needed to be wary. He figured he was safe-or so

he imagined.

****

Jeff Menke had no idea what hit him. He had been

thinking about Radka and knowing that he'd done her

wrong when at first he'd become aware of the smell. He'd

momentarily slowed his run to look around, and it was at

precisely that moment an immense, hairy hand came out of

the bushes and wrapped itself around his throat. He'd

struggled with all the strength he had when he'd seen Rad's

lifeless body thrown over the beast's opposite shoulder.

That bitch, Kate, had been right; it was Bigfoot. He

was a dead man. Jeff Menke simultaneously did two things:

he shit his pants and passed out.

****

Kretha was angry again. The man had fought him,

and he had to choke him. Kretha had choked many a

Clansman in his time and knew that the human would wake

soon, as would the female. He was, however, unprepared for what he was about to deal with. All morning he had allowed himself to be preoccupied with thoughts of the camp's other female. And now he was going to have to pay the price.

He had two humans who were not dead, but that was the least of his worries. He had allowed himself to be caught out in the open by one of the tree cutters and his Noise Maker. Kretha dropped the body of the man and prepared to advance upon the human in the Noise Maker when he caught sight of the Pain Stick and froze.

****

Jon Wilbur couldn't believe his eyes. Mother-fucking Bigfoot had just attacked a man and had a woman slung over his shoulder. Jon had always believed they were here, but never had he seen one, and he reckoned he never wanted to again.

He had no idea if the man and woman were alive, but that ugly damned beast was about to meet the business end of his 12 gauge. The beast dropped the man but still had the woman slung over his shoulder when he advanced upon the truck.

Standing on the running boards, he leveled the 12 gauge at the beast and pulled the trigger; he immediately racked the slide and chambered another round. Jon again pulled the trigger; he did this again and again until the gun was empty. All four rounds of buckshot hit the beast, but to Jon's horror, it also hit the woman, nearly cutting her in half.

He jumped back into the truck and slammed the door. As he was grabbing gears and revving the engine in terror, he could hear the beast's scream of rage.

****

The human in the Noise Maker had used the Pain Stick and thrown fire into him. He, the Chief of his Clan, was bitten time after time with the tiny balls of fire. The explosion from the first round of the Pain Stick had awakened the female slung over his shoulder, she immediately began screaming again. Kretha realized that the human's Pain Stick was biting into her as well. He tried to drop her, but again the Pain Stick exploded and the fire bit into his flesh. Once more the female screamed, and this time she jerked and shook, falling from his shoulder into his arms.

Her eyes, wide with terror and pain, gazed into his as once more the Pain Stick exploded and bit into both their flesh. Kretha watched as the light faded from the female's eyes. She had respected and honored him, and he had brought her to her death. Even though he had initially meant to kill her, he had changed his mind. He had felt the good in her.

The sting from the Pain Stick was fierce; it felt as if he was on fire. The body of the woman slid from his arms;

he could not have held her if he wanted to. Her shell was riddled with holes, and she was nearly cut in two pieces, her life blood, pouring out of her as her gaze stayed locked on his in death.

Kretha let out a scream of rage, and in complete violence, picked up the man who was just waking by his leg. The large machine was making noise but was unmoving; Kretha could see the human of death cowering inside.

He flung the man through the air toward the human hiding inside his Noise Maker. The man flew through the air, his screams echoing against the mountain, competing with Kretha's own.

The female's mate quit screaming as his body exploded through the front of the Noise Maker. Kretha had always thought the front of the Noise Maker was made of ice, but as the man's body shattered the barrier, he realized it must be something stronger, better. The human evaporated into a spray of red mist as he came to rest inside the Noise Maker.

Over the loud machine, Kretha could still hear screaming and knew that the man of death must still be alive inside.

The giant beast leapt to the Noise Maker and pummeled his fists into the hard surface. He grasped the only thing he could find and pulled, making an opening. Within, he saw the man of death sitting in a pool of blood and white bone from the female's mate. In a fit of rage, the Leviathan jumped to the trailer of the truck and began tearing at the timber wedged within its enclosure, finally loosening the trees.

One by one, he threw them, some landing on the road, others impaling themselves up to six feet into the earth, once again, standing upright.

Inside he could still hear the man's screams and could take it no longer; he would exact revenge. He *reached inside, pulled the old man from his seat, and*

dangled him off the ground by his head. The beast then

roared and flung the man onto the tree hauler where he

came to rest, impaled on what the beast only knew to be his

death stake.

****

Jon Wilbur watched in horror as the beast dropped the woman and picked up the man who was clearly still living. His eyes wide with terror, he tried putting the truck in gear but was too befuddled.

The beast flung the man through the air as if he weighed nothing, and with a bone-crunching, glass-shattering explosion, the man liquefied onto Jon's lap. He began screaming and didn't stop. He watched the beast approach and smash his fists into the hood, and then he tore off the door. Jon cowered in fear but was in shock and could not move.

The huge beast jumped up onto the trailer and began throwing off the logs that he'd, just hours earlier, loaded in the dark. The logs were flying everywhere, again Jon tried to put the truck in gear and get away, but his hands only trembled. He knew he continued to scream but couldn't seem to stop. Just when he thought it was over, the beast reached inside the cab and pulled him free.

Jon felt his skull crushing under the force of the monster's grip; he felt his body being flung through the air. He had a moment to register that he was much too close to the metal trailer bunks when he felt his body begin its decent onto them.

Jon Wilbur was alive for several minutes, his lungs slowly filling with blood, drowning him. He tried thinking of the Lord's Prayer or anything else that may ease his way into Heaven, but nothing came to mind as he stared down into the bowels of Hell.

****

Kretha was enraged as he watched the man of death die. His blood gurgled out of his mouth. When he was sure he was dead, he went back to the female and rested his hand upon her heart. He was sorry her end had come this way.

He would return to his Clan and gather his hunters; he would bring along Goya as well. His heir must learn that humans were to be looked upon as bringers of death!

Together they would return to the female's camp and kill them all. Kretha would take the female and find out how she had entered his mind, and when he knew her secret, he would end her life, too.

As he ran toward his Clan, he watched for signs that he neared, and upon seeing the first, he issued the first battle cry. His warriors must be ready. They would not like the deed that was to be done; it was against the Laws of the Leviathans to kill a human, but Kretha had broken it several times today, and he would kill any of his own kind

that dare oppose him now.

When he entered the camp of the Clan, his warriors

stood ready

Chapter Thirteen

Kate had no idea that even as she was calling for help, that assistance was already enroute. Cole Roberts and Dylan Thomas met Joe at the trailhead, and together they were only a few minutes behind Red and his warriors. All three men were heavily armed and prepared for the worst.

Each man having something completely different on his mind, Joe simply wanted to get to Kate and make sure she was safe. He wanted to tell her how sorry he was and how stupid.

Cole Roberts knew that Dylan would have his back, but he also worried about the brother of his new wife. Dylan was a badass, and Cole had no idea if he knew his own limitations. Somewhere deep in his heart, Cole was terrified; he'd survived an ordeal a year ago, and he knew what was happening then. At this point, he knew nothing other than Kate had called Mari.

Dylan Thomas knew what he was up against. He always knew and was always prepared. Last year when Mari had been on a mountain not too far from here, he had been pretty much helpless to save her. She'd saved herself, and he knew Kate Mitchell had the balls to do the same thing.

This time was different for Dylan, though; it wasn't his sister, and he knew exactly what he was going to be facing down. He was locked, cocked, and ready to rock. He knew every day that when a call came in and he got called away from his family, that it might not end well.

As he and Mari liked to say, "Shit might get ugly," but if it did, then he would be as prepared as a man could be. He knew that even though he traveled with two other men, both of whom he called friends when shit hit the fan; he was a one-man demolition crew. Dylan had no problems when people laughed and joked that he was not armed and dangerous, but armed and considerably dangerous. It was who he was born and bred to be. He had every intention of going home.

****

Khryl and his warriors were two miles away from Merr-ee's friend. They were traveling fast and knew that death was in the air. The Chief and his three warriors could smell the blood, so it was no surprise when they detoured slightly and found the corpse of the man buried in a shallow grave. The man who sheltered several valleys over was an odd one; Khryl had never sensed no trouble from him.

Khryl had known of his existence, but the man had not come into his Clan's territory. His watchers had reported that the man was touched in the head, and they had ignored him.

The Chief worried that they would be too late to save the group of people whom Merr-ee had sent him for. He also worried that his own warriors would be injured.

Khryl questioned his skills and rightful place as the Clan's Chief. He should have personally come here to these mountains and requested a gathering with this Clan; he had not, and he feared more humans would die from his lack of vigilance.

Had Churel taught him nothing? It was times like this that he dearly missed the mighty Thor. Rooba was a strong and honorable warrior, but Thor was a true giant among giants. Many times back at the great waters, just the sight of Thor would send another Clan on their way.

It was too late now. Khryl had a job to do and it would be done. Merr-ee and her people had protected his Clan, and Khryl owed her mate, Kooal. Churel had hunted the man and killed his friend.

The Chief knew that his humans did not believe there was a debt to be repaid, but Khryl believed that Merr-ee and Kooal were a part of his Clan now, and that meant any trouble they came across was now his as well.

****

Kate and the campers had built up the fire and taken stock of what they had. She'd pulled Ben in from the perimeter, and he and Blake kept a constant vigil over the camp while she'd called in reinforcements. Richard was still in shock, but the kid was doing his best, she would give him that. He had made sure there was plenty of food and water ready to go.

Kate had put out the Mayday signal and knew that both her dad and Jace would be informed. Mari had taken the call and assured her that help was already on the way and to evacuate the area immediately via the trail they had come in on. There was conflicting views as to what needed to happen.

Kate was inclined to listen to Mari and leave immediately, but she'd received radio contact from some head honcho at the Forest Service telling her to stand down and maintain her last known position. That she did not know what had happened to the missing people—only a presumed animal attack—had the Feds pissy and threatening to pull licensing if she didn't maintain her position so a search and rescue operation could be initiated.

She had just glanced at her watch. It was shortly past noon, and she'd instructed everyone to eat. The ATVs were ready to go, and Kate had decided that the Forest Service could go to hell. They were leaving.

"Listen up, people. We are leaving at 12:30 on the dot. Blake, you will lead, and behind you, I want Mimi and Marley on the big 800. Mimi, if anything happens, you ride and do not stop. Richard, you will follow her and make sure she is not followed. Ben, you and I will flank the entire bunch. Anyone have questions?"

"Kate? You heard what the Forest Service said. I will stay." This comment from Blake.

"I am not sure you heard what I just said, Blake. Unless you choose to no longer work for me, then you are leading this group outta hear in exactly ten minutes. As for the Forest Service, they can take their licenses and shove them up their asses; I no longer give two fucks. Does that clear up any confusion for you? So, I guess the question is, if you work for me or not?"

"I can't leave them, Kate; what if they come back wounded or just scared?"

"Well, I can't force you, Blake. I am sorry you feel that way, and I think we both know that you're wishful thinking. Ben, you're taking the lead. Everyone else, nothing changes."

"C'mon, Kate, please. Mari said help was coming; shit, we both know that means fucking Joe is on his way to rescue you, and Dylan Thomas is probably armed to his balls as well. I'd bet that Cole is on his way up here as well. The Forest Service said they'd have someone here shortly. We can hold this thing off. Don't go out there," Blake pleaded with her.

Kate stared at him for a moment. Taken aback by the "fucking Joe is on his way to rescue you" remark, she finally understood the depth of his feelings for her and felt guilty that she couldn't reciprocate them. She also knew he was being a fool by staying and that if she agreed to hang out here, she'd be putting the lives of all these other people at risk. She was feeling shitty enough for having stereotyped both the Menke's from the get-go, but the bottom line was she was damn good at her job and knew this area, and something was wrong.

She'd seen it. She'd known it was there, and she knew it was coming back. What scared her most was she was positive that it was coming for her.

Kate was shaking her head and just getting ready to tell him no when not just one but several screams broke the silence. It was too damn late. They were surrounded, and *if* help was coming, it wasn't here yet, and now was when she needed it most. *Damn you, Joe, where were you? Was he even coming?*

****

Khryl and the warriors that traveled with him heard the screams tear through the afternoon and knew them to be the cries of battle. They were close, but they could not make it in time. They ran at a pace that would stop a man's heart to just witness. One year ago, three of these same warriors ran like this; only this time, their Chief was at their side. Just like then, birds took to the skies, animals that had holes dove into them, and the hoofed creatures ran as if the Hounds of Hell were baying at their heels. The ground shook and the trees swayed.

****

A mile behind the beasts, the three men felt the disturbance in the air moments after they heard the distant screams and knew what was happening. They'd all been there a year before. They knew the disturbance was Red and his hunters going to Kate; they knew that she needed the giants now more than ever, but what they didn't know was how far away they were and if they would make it in time to save her.

To their credit, none of the three men faltered in pace even though they knew what was going to happen. Dylan had the best ATV and quickly pulled away from the others, if they were honest, it would be Red, his warriors and Dylan that saved Kate anyway. Joe and Cole Roberts pushed on as fast as they could, both fearing the worst.

****

Dylan Thomas could smell the beasts in front of him. He had made it a point of learning their scent. Usually he could tell who was in the forest with him, and today he had no trouble discerning that it was Red and the three hunters he called Rooba, Cro and Zon.

He knew he couldn't outrun them, but he wouldn't be far behind either. As he came over a rise, he saw the four giants just ahead; they were startling in their ability to run through the woods given their size. He saw Red glance back, and the Bigfoot that his sister Mari had taken it upon herself to claim as a personal pet nodded and indicated that Dylan should proceed with them.

He gave the machine the last bit of throttle it had in it and prepared for battle. This time it would be different; he had no idea how many they would be up against, and he had to keep in mind that four of them were friendlies.

He'd already discussed with Cole and Joe that if there were survivors, their job was to get them out. Dylan's job was to fight alongside Red. Mari had told Kate what to expect, and he hoped like hell she didn't open fire on Red because that would just piss him the fuck off.

Chapter Fourteen

Kate had told everyone what Mari had told her. Every camper knew what was there waiting for them, and they also knew that coming from the safety of the trail were three men and some other creatures that Mari called "friendly."

Kate was strictly forbidden to shoot any that appeared to help, more specifically one that was Red. Kate wished that she had taken the time to call her dad and Jace. They might never know what had happened up here if she died.

Hell, she thought, *there was no damn way she was going to die.*

The screams had come from all around camp and at a distance she would guess to be about seventy-five yards. Not a perfect range for a pistol or shotgun, but she instructed the group to place their shots well and save their ammo.

She'd had Blake and Ben light small fires around the perimeter of the camp, and thanked God that Richard had moved the food trailer in closer, offering a little shelter. He was to protect Mimi and Marley. The screaming continued but stayed in place, however the ground seemed to shake. Kate looked around; the skies were full of birds, it seemed surreal, but animals were running everywhere. She had no idea what was happening and didn't have to wait long to find out.

The first boulder was launched into camp, smashing into the food trailer that everyone was using as shelter. Kate screamed at them not to scatter, and they didn't.

She heard a gunshot and another roar. Marley was screaming, and so was Richard, but Kate didn't want to take her eyes off the forest. She heard Mimi trying to soothe Marley and telling Richard to breathe and that he would okay. Shit, was he wounded?

Kate glanced at the trio and saw Richard lying on his back, his right shin bone torn through his jeans, blood pooling around his leg. Mimi still huddled over Marley but had taken her jacket and was trying to stop the blood with it. The boulder that had hit the cook trailer ricocheted off and landed on Richard's leg.

Kate turned away; there was nothing she could do for him but try to keep whatever was trying to kill them away. She heard a whistling and hit the ground just as a ten-foot-long green spruce tree tore into the side of the cook trailer right where she'd been moments before. The trailer listed to the side.

"Blake! Ben!" she screamed.

"We're okay!" Blake responded. "How's Richard?"

"Not good, compound fracture. Otherwise, we're okay over here."

"What do we do, Kate? Mimi? You okay, babe?"

"I'm fine, Ben." The woman yelled in response.

"I suggest we each shoot one round at intervals of five seconds. Try to shoot wisely. Am I the only one who can't see shit?" Kate replied.

"They're too far into the timber to see. What do you think about placing our shots in the directions the screams are and where the shit is being thrown from? I think there are four or five of them." Ben replied.

"I agree," said Blake

"Mimi, I need you to put Marley to your back and lay down fire, okay?" Kate told the woman.

"Yup, I'm on it. I've got Rich as far under the trailer as I can, and I have his gun," the young woman replied. Kate smiled.

"Okay, guys, thanks for manning up; you're the best two campers I've ever had. Now, let's get this done. I'll start, and on a five count, Ben, you shoot and so forth. Everyone got it? Marley, you stay low, okay, honey?"

Kate sat up and aimed the shotgun directly were the spruce had come from and pulled the trigger. Her shot was met with an immediate roar of pain. Her companions whooped. "Not so fast, guys, doesn't mean anything. And remember, aim a little left or right each round; I think these bastards are smart and are gonna catch on. You're up, Ben."

They went around the trailer, and in eight rounds, they were met with two more growls. Unfortunately, the growls were getting closer and closer. They'd parked the

ATVs in positions to hopefully aid in cover, but when Kate heard Blake swear, she knew they were in trouble.

"Shoot, Ben! Jesus, shoot!" he cried. Everyone was kneeling or sitting behind something for protection, but when Kate was thrown forward onto her face, her shotgun skidding out of her hand, she was momentarily stunned.

The sound of twisting metal landed right in front of her, she cautiously lifted her head and saw one of her ATVs lying in a heap. She was momentarily confused, however, because it looked like someone had wrapped white paper around it. It hit her that what she was seeing was part of the cook trailer tangled within it. She glanced over her shoulder, and where the trailer once stood was nothing but a frame and four tires.

Mimi stared around wild-eyed, her body on top of Marley's; Richard was deathly white. Too white in fact. The boy wasn't among the living.

Ben was crawling toward Mimi, and Blake was nowhere to be seen.

"Blake?" she whispered.

"No, Kate," said Ben, blood dribbling down his face from a cut somewhere on his head. He just shook his head and looked toward the wrecked ATV.

Kate looked again at the mangled mess ten feet from her and saw a hand. She crawled toward it and grabbed her shotgun as she went. She tore away the sheet metal expecting to find Blake underneath, but recoiled in horror when all that was there were his hand and a small portion of his arm. "What the hell?" she cried.

Scrambling away from the wreckage, she propelled herself backward and saw Blake's once handsome face. The face of one of her best friends, coworkers and confidants tangled in the wreckage that was at one time his own ATV.

She closed her eyes and breathed deeply; the fucking monster had thrown the ATV into him and the trailer.

Her friend was in God damn pieces! A lesser woman would have collapsed, but Kate Mitchell rose to all five feet nine inches and yelled into the timber, "I told you I would kill you! I fucking told you!"

She stood there staring off into space, knowing exactly what she was seeing and to whom her thoughts were directed. "You are dead, do you understand me, you filthy fucking beast? I will hunt you down and kill you if it's the last thing I do! And I swear to God I will take your head as my trophy."

****

From fifty yards away hidden within the timber, Kretha, the mighty Chief, felt the female come once again inside his head. He knew exactly what she said. It was if she spoke the language of the Leviathans. He must capture and kill her; she had wounded his heir.

Goya would survive, but father and son were both stinging from the bite of the humans' Fire Sticks today, and it was because of this female. He should have never let her stay. Now she was inside his head; her voice was like a snake hissing from within, and it angered and scared the Chief. She would be dealt with, but first a new threat had arrived.

The Clan from across the mountains had come and interfered with his war. That could never be tolerated.

****

Kate felt the beast; he was injured, as was his son. She didn't know how she knew, but she did, and she refused to let the connection go. She also knew that Mari's reinforcements were here. She chose to step forward and yell again.

"I know you feel me! I know you're wounded, as is your child. I will kill him too! And I will take both of your heads! Do not mistake my words, beast, I am coming for you!" With that last statement, she threw back her head and laughed, pointed directly at the beast, raised her shotgun and unloaded it, not knowing or caring if any of the buckshot hit home, only knowing that she would never ever allow him to live.

****

Kretha recoiled in horror! The female had advanced upon him; she knew where he hid. At first her threat to Goya enraged him and even scared him, but it was when she had pointed at him, laughed and then raised the Pain Stick that she had held him immobile. It was only as her stinging fireballs ripped into already wounded flesh that he fled. He forgot the battle that raged behind him; his warriors were losing to the Clan from across the mountains. There was another Noise Maker—several, actually. One was coming fast, and just as he knew the female had special powers, he knew he must flee this Noise Maker or die.

****

Khryl had not arrived in time to stop all the destruction, but the Chief knew there were survivors within the camp. He and his three hunters found that the humans had wounded several of the other Clan's warriors and were making short work of exterminating the renegades. There would be no exceptions this time, and death was the only option to harming a human.

Khryl knew that Merr-ee's sibling was also fighting and looked to make sure he was safe; the sibling of Merr-ee was killing a particularly large male and having no problems doing it. Khryl knew the man would be fine. In the distance he heard two Noise Makers coming up the hill and scented the air. It was Kooal and another man that

Khryl remembered from last summer. Closer, however, a Noise Maker was starting, and it was coming toward them. He again scented the air and found it to be Merr-ee's friend and was pleased that she lived.

As the Noise Maker advanced upon the battle, Khryl put himself on guard as he did not know if Merr-ee's friend would find him to be her enemy.

When the female entered the clearing, she stopped and stepped off the Noise Maker. Khryl was astonished to see the rage on her face. She looked toward the sibling of Merr-ee and around the clearing where bodies of several Leviathans lay. Khryl stood in the middle and she zeroed in on him. The Chief was immediately aware that she carried two Pain Sticks. As she neared him, she looked him in the eye and spoke to his mind without using words. Taken aback, Khryl snorted thus attracting Rooba's attention.

****

"I am Kate Mitchell. Thank you for coming. Mari said you were Red and that you were a friend. I seek the Chief of this Clan and his child. The Chief is Kretha, his son is Goya, and I have come to take their heads. Are they here?" Kate spoke her words out loud even though she knew that the Bigfoot, Mari called Red, could understand.

Dylan Thomas approached her and looked at her with an odd look. For Dylan, an odd look meant he was uncomfortable or confused, and Kate knew that to be a rarity.

"Kate, glad you're okay. Looks like your people did some good work here. How many did you lose?"

"Two for sure, but I am assuming the missing man and woman are dead as well. Both my guides are dead back at camp. Daughter of the missing man and woman and a young couple that had their shit together is all that is left."

"Blake's gone?" Dylan looked at Kate, completely floored that his friend had been killed.

"Yes, Dylan, I know he was your friend, too." She looked at him briefly then turned her attention to the giant red beast. "Now I know Red here can understand every damned word I am saying. So, where are they? The Chief, Kretha, and his son, Goya. I want them, Dylan, and I want them right this fucking minute."

Kate looked from Dylan to Red who had been joined by Rooba. Cro and Zon were dragging the four dead bodies away to be buried, but they, too, stopped at her words.

"Uh, Kate, you mind telling me how you know who the Chief of the Clan is and who his cub is, and how the hell you're communicating with them? Red looks like he is either going to shit himself or eat you, and Mari isn't going to like either."

"Hell if I know, Dylan. It just happened this morning. I knew; I felt it, I felt him, and I still feel it. I heard his thoughts just like I can hear Red's thoughts. And if Red's bodyguard doesn't settle his shit, I'm gonna turn him into a fucking Bigfoot meatloaf." Kate directed her thoughts at Red who immediately grunted at the other one and motioned him away.

"Christ, Kate, are you like Bigfoot psychic or some shit?"

"Really, Dylan, how the hell should I know? All I know is that one of my best friends is dead, and that hairy fuck is planning to kill me, so I think you of all people can understand how it's game on."

"Yeah, yeah, I gotcha, Kate. Uh, Red, this is Kate, Kate, this is Red. Let's not have any killing between friends, okay? Mari would be upset."

"I introduced myself, Dylan. He heard me. Didn't you, Red? Nod your big-ass hairy head. Like this." Kate bobbed her head up and down, but there was no need; Mari had been teaching Red the basics for a year.

"*Yes,*" he responded with a very guttural sound.

"See, Dylan, I told you. Now let's get this show on the road. Can you track him if I can sense his thoughts?" She directed her question at Dylan, but Red interrupted again.

"*Yes, I can track them, as can my hunters*" In her head the giant responded as if that was all the explanation Kate needed. She didn't want or need any more clarification. At least the hairy shit would be good for something.

"Hmm, not a bad idea; especially coming from a flipping Bigfoot, what do you think, Dylan?" She repeated Red's words. "But first Ben, Mimi, and Marley need to get off this mountain. And I want my guides off, too. Make it happen."

"Jesus, Kate, bitch mode much? Ever heard the saying "you catch more flies with honey? Cole and Joe are coming. Probably at camp now, we should go back and make a plan." He glared at her and walked towards his ATV. Dylan flipped Kate the bird, if nothing else he wanted her to know who the boss was.

"Ya know what, Dylan? Fuck you, fuck Cole, and especially fuck Joe Roberts!" Her voice was rising. "You all knew what was up here, and you hid it from me, you pussy footed around the possible dangers, and none of you trusted me enough to keep the secret. All summer long I have been putting multiple lives in danger, lives of little kids, my own life because you all wanted to protect a stinking Bigfoot! I would not have ever said a word! But this was some definite need-to-know information!"

She was all but screaming at one of the most powerful men she'd ever met, but was beyond caring.

"I lost a relationship because Joe was too selfish to tell me! I nearly died because of it, and the parents of a little girl are most likely dead because of your secrets! Now I have to find the words to tell two families that their sons, my friends and employees, are dead because of those damn secrets! I suppose we're going to go with the whole killer grizzly thing again? I don't think so, Dylan; people have a right to know!"

Kate looked toward Red; she knew he understood. "I get what you and Red tried to do for me; in fact, I owe his big hairy ass. I have no idea how I am going to pay HIM back." She jerked her head in Khryls direction.

"Probably by keeping my mouth shut. But this was wrong of all of you to do to me. I would have simply moved the tours to a new location, but did any one of you ask yourself if I should know? Did you know there was another group?" She paused.

****

It was Red who entered her mind, "We left after last summer, but our hearts were here. We came back in the spring so I could find Merr-ee and Kooal. I suspected there was another Clan living in these mountains, but they kept to themselves. I posted my watchers, and they did not leave the valley. Merr-ee asked me to watch you, and this summer, my hunters did; the Clan never seemed interested. It is my fault this happened to you. Please do not blame your friends. I failed you, I failed Merr-ee. I will find and kill the Chief and this Goya you seek. I do not know what the other humans in your camp will do, but I ask that you not bring forth more humans onto my side of the mountain where my Clan resides."

****

Kate was momentarily speechless by Red's words. "Thank you, Red; I appreciate your telling me the truth. I also appreciate you offering to complete this hunt for me, but I finish what I start, and this is personal. I intend to keep my mouth shut, but I don't know what the Forest Service will discover up here. I have no idea what the people back at my camp saw or what they will say. They know we believe it was Bigfoot that harassed us, but quite frankly, I am too tired to care. I need for them to be taken to safety. But I intend to continue."

Kate spun on her heels and stopped in her tracks. Behind her stood Joe, the man she loved, or rather at this exact moment, the man she loved to hate. He had heard every word she'd said, and she didn't care.

"Kate, I'm so sorry." Joe's face was white, yet underneath it, he felt himself smiling at the sight of his Katie. His grin widened as she walked toward him.

Kate had no idea what she was going to say, but what came out was not at all what either of them expected: a close-fisted punch right to the face. Once she was mid swing, she discovered how good it felt and put her weight behind it for the proper carry through. Screw Joe and his apologies; she had a Bigfoot or two to kill.

She hopped on her four wheeler and rode back to camp where Cole was on his Sat phone probably discussing how to hide this mess under the heading "Killer Grizzly Strikes Again." For good measure, she should kick his ass, too, but that would just upset Mari. Kate knew that what they had done was the right thing; it just pissed her off that not one of them had told her the truth.

Chapter Fifteen

Kate stood staring into the timber, Dylan Thomas next to her, and together they discussed the plan. Kate had spoken to Ben and Mimi, and although both were upset, neither one had any idea what had *really* waged the attack. Or so they said. Kate thought it was probably their way of staying out of the mess. Plus, she knew Cole had been alone with them for quite some time before she'd gotten back to camp. They were going to take Marley back to base camp where her dad and brother waited. Everyone believed that Kate, Dylan, and Joe were waiting for the Forest Service who had still yet to arrive.

Red and his hunters had scouted ahead and found the other Clan. It did seem like, as a whole, they were peaceful and lived in constant fear of their leader. Khryl had offered the small group of females and cubs asylum within his Clan if they were to sever all ties with their Chief.

Kate listened in on the conversation and was shocked to hear that one of the Bigfoot refugees—so to speak—was the renegade's own mate and his female cub.

Ravana and Kali were more than willing to escape Kretha and join Khryls Clan. It would appear that Mari and Cole would soon have more of these things than they bargained for to protect. She had kept Dylan informed of what was happening, and since she wasn't speaking to Joe, Dylan had let him in on Kate's newly developed abilities.

Joe was none too pleased and tried to demand Kate leave, but one look from her and the reminder that what he wanted didn't mean shit to her, he shut his mouth.

Kate hugged Marley and promised the little girl she would look for her mama, but Kate knew that when and if they found Radka Menke, she would be dead. The girl never once asked about her father, and Kate thought that was probably for the best; she presumed him to be lost as well.

As the group prepared to leave, Ben offered his assistance one last time, Kate hated to see him go but knew the right thing for him to do was to take his fiancée and leave this mountain.

She had grossly underestimated both he and Mimi and would do whatever it took to make it right with them down the road, should she survive. She'd known what the outcome could be to this and had called and talked to her dad and Jace; neither needed to know the absolute truth, but she wanted to be sure they knew how much she loved them and that if something did go wrong with the "Grizzly," that this was her area, and Blake and Rich had been her responsibilities.

They had taken the news about Blake's death hard and were equally saddened by Rich's. God, she'd been a real bitch to the kid, but Kate knew in the end he'd stepped up and protected Mimi and the kid, and she made sure that everyone knew he'd died a hero. It did little to ease her conscience, but what was done was done; she could take none of it back.

****

Kate knew that the Chief, Kretha, was wounded and that he'd waged war. She also knew that she'd wounded him further in her last tirade, but the farther he traveled away, the less she could pick up. She could feel the offspring more clearly and knew that he had taken shelter in a cave not far from here. She had kept the knowledge to herself for the moment and intended to carry out her threat to kill him later.

Kate tried desperately to project her thoughts so that if Kretha was listening, he would hear; she knew the young male was listening and could feel his fear. She supposed that a kinder, gentler woman such as Mari would attempt to reform the young beast, but within his mind she felt a strong bond with his father.

The heir to the Clan was confused as to why his father had abandoned him to the humans; more especially, why had he left him to the female who touched his mind?

Kate grinned inside at the young male's anguish and continued to project.

"You followed your father; you made a choice to attack me and mine when we had done nothing to harm you and yours. Vengeance will be mine, and you know it to be so. I will have your head, young Goya. You can hide, you can run, but you can never escape me. I am Kate, and I am to be your killer. I know you understand everything I say to you. Do your Clan the honor of standing down. If you make me come for you, I will chase you to the ends of the earth, and for that, your punishment will not only be death, but I will take your head. I know the Laws of the Leviathans; I know you must never kill a human. You have broken that law. I know that the Leviathans bury their dead and perform a ritual; I will ensure your body be treated with respect, but I demand you stand down and come to me. Your punishment will still be death, as you know, but if you disobey me, young one, I will own you. Once I have your head, I will take it as I hunt your father, and before I kill him, he will know of your death and of your failure as his heir. I promise you I will throw your head at his feet, and together you will never reach the Heavens. Khryl, the great Chief who has given your Clan sanctuary, has told me of the ways. I know you will be doomed to Hell if your burial rituals are not performed. I know, Goya that you merely followed your bastard of a father's command, but I feel it in your heart that you are confused by his treachery and lies. You still honor your father, and I respect that as I honor my father, but your father is a cruel and heartless killer of humans. Do not make me chase you, for your death will not be swift."

Kate again smiled into the darkening timber as the sun was starting its decent for the day. She had hoped that she would be able to start her mission before now, but the cover of darkness was her friend. Especially now that she could hear her enemies' murderous thoughts, Kate knew the shadows would be her friend.

One of Red's beasts traveled with Cole and her campers back to safety. Another led Kretha's Clan across the mountains to join his kind. That left her with Dylan, Joe, Red, and the warrior who watched her the closest; she had heard Red call him Rooba.

Kate was careful to keep some of her thoughts to herself, but she knew Rooba had listened in on her one-sided conversation with Goya. She'd felt him stiffen, but he'd remained silent knowing that everything she'd projected was the truth and simply directed at Goya and not at him or his Chief.

She could not help herself, though, and without turning from the woods, said to Rooba.

"Hello, Rooba, I know I must shock and probably appall you. You are not quite comfortable around humans yet, are you? It is okay, I understand. If I'm honest, I am not comfortable around them either. I wish to say I'm sorry that you have been brought into this. Your Chief told me about last summer, and what he didn't, I heard in the thoughts of the rest of you. I am sorry for your loss. Rest assured, though, it is not my intent to tell your secret or invade your privacy. I do not even wish for you to be here. I have a mission to carry out, and I will see it through. The Chief, Kretha, and his cub as you call them, waged a war on me and mine. We did nothing to provoke it, and two special people are dead—probably more—and not only can I not let that go, but Kretha intends to come back and kill me. I hope you understand that I respect your species, but my life is just as important as yours." Kate ended her thoughts by looking over her shoulder at the beast that stood in the shadows.

When she was sure he was looking at her, she nodded at him and put her hand on her heart for a brief moment and looked away.

****

Rooba had been faced with several challenges in his life. Last year he had knowingly forgiven his friend Thor for eating a man out of starvation, and then in a moment of desperation, Thor had nearly taken the life of the Chief's human female. He had pledged his allegiance to the Chief many seasons ago and believed that Khryl was the best Chief any warrior could have. Where the Chief went, he followed; he had become the Chief's protector whether he wanted it or not.

Earlier he had feared this powerful woman; he had no idea how she was able to put her human voice inside his kinds' heads, and it was terrifying, but his Chief had stood and listened as only Khryl would do.

Khryl had shared with the female the Clan's history and Rooba had watched her closely. The Leviathans had lived for millennia believing that humans must be avoided and that to be detected meant certain death. Khryl had proven that wrong and they had lived a good life here in these mountains.

Finally, their bellies were full, and their mates were producing cubs as they should be. They were flourishing. He trusted in his Chief.

The female had spoken to him with her mind; he had heard her calling out to the other Chief's heir and knew she intended to hunt him.

Rooba didn't know that there were humans able to use Mind Speak; the Leviathans were able to communicate among themselves, but to have a human inside his head was unsettling. He had listened to her speaking to the one she called Goya and realized that she was no different than he or his Chief in wanting to end the renegade and willing to do so in a manner that was acceptable to their beliefs.

She had given him a chance to honor his Clan; he knew what his punishment would be, and the female had explained the alternative. She was not out of line. When she had spoken to him, she had apologized for bringing him and his Clan into her war, and that touched Rooba. He now understood how Khryl was able to form such an attachment to his human. The female had pledged her respect and allegiance to him by placing her hand over her heart. Rooba would not quickly forget that.

He knew this female was hardened and sad from her losses. He had seen the destruction left by the Chief,

Kretha, and his warriors. It was inexcusable and no different than what Churel had done last summer.

He knew the female called herself Kate, and he knew she had a plan. He wondered if he could block his thoughts from her and observe her. Rooba suspected that Kate was going to get into trouble and his Chief would be honor-bound to protect his human's friend. That is why they were here after all. Therefore, it would become Rooba's job to watch this new female so his Chief stayed safe. First though, he would try to reach her and see if she would open herself to him; it would be easier if she let him help her. He was the largest beast in the forest, and not even her mind could escape that fact.

"Female, it is I, Rooba, who wishes to speak to you. You call yourself Kate, and you are able to Mind Speak, yes?"

****

Kate bristled when she heard Rooba's words in her head. But answered regardless, "Yes, I am Kate, and it appears I am able to do this thing you call Mind Speak. What is it you want with me? I told you I wish you no harm."

****

"I, too, wish no harm to come to you. I heard you calling to the one you call Goya. I did not hear him. He is too far for me. Your Mind Speak is powerful, human. I fear that you will only bring harm to yourself. Even wounded, the cub is powerful, and the Chief, Kretha, will be enraged if you kill his heir. I plead with you to allow us, the Leviathans, to handle this. I shall help you. I understand your need for revenge, human, but you cannot win this.

Even with your plan to steal the sibling of Merr-ee's Pain Stick, you will not survive. You may well need the sibling of Merr-ee and his Pain Stick to survive, but you

will for sure need me."

****

"Ah, so you can hear my thoughts as well, I see. I must try harder to block what I am thinking. I had guessed you would be a problem, Rooba. I will consider your offer as it would be foolish of me to anger you, and I can obviously see where you would be an asset to my cause. But you must know I am not pleased to have you intrude on my revenge, and I sense that you will sell me out if I do not agree to allow you to assist me. Am I wrong, Rooba? You will tell your Chief of my plans if I do not agree?"

****

"You are a very smart and wise human. I see now why Khryl has chosen to bring your kind so closely into our Clan. I find that I like your warrior spirit, Kate, and do not wish you dead. I would be remiss if I did not tell my Chief

of your plans one way or the other, and that I cannot do.

My allegiance will always be with my Chief. I can,

however, help you. My Chief has a duty to his Merr-ee, to

keep you safe. My duty is to keep my Chief safe. Do you

understand? I will allow you to proceed with your plan,

human, but only until I feel that you are a danger to

yourself or to my Chief."

****

"I won't even pretend to know what you mean,

Rooba, and I don't pretend to give a shit either. I am not

settled on what my plan is, and if you're around when I put

it into action, then so be it. But understand one thing, beast:

I will not, under any circumstances, allow you to get in my

way. If I die, then it is my God's will. Do not try to impede

me. You think Dylan Thomas is a scary son of a bitch? You

have not seen me truly pissed off. If you want to do anyone

a favor, do Mari and Cole the favor by keeping Joe alive."

She paused for effect. "If one of your kind doesn't get him, and I am still undecided here, but there's a good chance I might end him myself." With that she turned to stare at Rooba full on for a moment and walked off. She had shit to prepare and intended to block that nosy asshole from her mind.

****

Chapter Sixteen

Kretha was enraged and struggling against the pain surging through his body. The Pain Sticks had opened hundreds of tiny holes that oozed blood; he knew he would heal quickly and just needed to find nourishment and the proper roots before they became infected. It was, however, the pain within his mind and heart that hurt the worst: having the female constantly within his mind. Just when he thought he'd escaped her, she'd push through and he'd hear her and the things she was saying to poor Goya!

When he was well, he would kill her and rescue Goya. He only hoped that his son and heir would hold out and not submit to her. How dare she threaten to kill him and take his head! Kretha would never allow it, but he must pray to the Gods that Goya was strong enough and not wounded badly enough to give in to her demands. The female was powerful; that could not be denied.

Kretha was outraged that his Clan had deserted him as well. They had taken refuge across the mountains with the Clan that had slaughtered their mates, fathers, and siblings.

He had always ruled his Clan with an iron fist and to the letter of the Great Law, but this was inexcusable. He would punish them, but the first thing he must do was find food and water. He had traveled far to get away from the female and her Mind Speak. Never had he encountered a human with her power. He berated himself now for not having run her off years ago or killed the humans this morn.

He was a fool, and he hoped he would not further be punished for his stupidity.

He was searching for berries when he heard the sound of human voices. He did not recognize the voices or their scent, but he was in a new and unfamiliar territory.

Kretha was not completely sure where he was, only that he could follow his own trail home if need be.

As quickly and quietly as a giant of his size could, he hid within the shrubs and timber. He realized he had fled up a human dirt path; his mistakes kept mounting as did his anger and frustration.

At least here, he was free from the female rooting around inside his head. He could no longer hear Goya's pleading either, which was both a sorrow and a relief.

The voices were coming closer, but he remained silent and still, a thought coming to him. Why not? He struggled to block the images of the people he'd killed from the female, but why not allow her to see exactly what he was going to do to her? She had threatened to take his Goya's head and drop it at his feet and then take his, had she not?

There were at least two humans coming, and he would kill them and take their heads. He would purposely move down the mountain and open himself to her so she could see what he had done to them, including the old man early this morning, and end with the two heads he would carry as his gift for her!

He could see them now; how lucky that it was two females! Both with the same long white hair that the female had; it was perfect. Meant to be, a gift from the Gods. He waited, wanting there to be no chance of escape or for them to have a Pain Stick. He would surprise the humans and take them both at once.

Kretha's heart beat faster in his chest and his lips parted on a snarl of excitement. He must remain silent, but he would enjoy the moment nonetheless.

As the females approached, he sprang up from the bushes and flung his arms wide. They both stopped frozen in their tracks, neither uttering a word, shocked into silence. In one powerful lunge, he sprang onto the trail and landed right in front of the females. Without even thinking, he slammed their heads together, pleased at the sickening crunch of bone. Blood sprayed out of both their noses and mouths. Their eyes bulged out of the sockets from the impact, brains exploding the second their skulls made contact. Neither felt a thing.

Pleased with himself, he wrapped one hand around each neck and flicked as if it was nothing more than a pesky mosquito, their heads easily popped free. The bodies collapsed lifeless to the ground where blood quickly pooled out of their open necks.

Grabbing the heads by the hair, he sprang once again off the trail and sprinted down the mountain, gathering what berries he could shove in his mouth. At the first stream he came to, he drank deeply and chewed some Bloodroot to ease his pain. He stuffed the masticated leaves into his many wounds and felt immediate relief. He rested briefly and opened his mind to the female.

****

Deb and her friend had traveled two thousand miles to hike in freaking fabulous Montana. She had spent nearly thirty years hearing about how wonderful this God forsaken hellhole was, and frankly, she was already sick of the shit; traipsing through the jungle with grizzlies and killer mosquitoes was pissing her off.

She was feeling sorry for herself and her pathetic life. She'd just went through an ugly divorce, her grown daughters were of their own mind, and she really didn't give two shits about them.

Deb had married a fat, disgusting pig of a man the moment her divorce was final, but what really stung was that her teenage son refused to have anything to do with her. All this drama and bullshit over $1,700 in DVDs.

Deb had begged her closest friend, Julie, to come on this trip with her just to rub it in Thomas' face. She knew how much he loved this shit hole, and she'd used his money and left the fat pig at home to come on what she considered her "Divorce Vacation." At the time, it seemed like just the perfect way to rub it in his gloating face. He was making it big time in his band, and she was schlepping horse shit.

She hated it here and was glad that she'd never bothered to come before now. Her hatred of life oozed off her like a disease. She couldn't help it if the dentist who had done her teeth after her go with Meth had infected her with Hep C. Her life sucked and she'd done it to herself. From the frying pan, straight to the fire she thought.

Deb was already clueless and considered stupid as shit, but when the creature stepped out and bashed her head in, she became headless as well. What brains she had seeped from her shattered skull.

Her eyeballs hung by the sinew that kept them in their sockets, and her once round head was flattened. It was the perfect end, to a pathetic existence.

Of course, no one would ever know what happened to the cheating whore. It didn't help that the creature disposed well of his kill and took her flattened head as a trophy. Sadly, Deb had felt her skull collapse against the force of smashing into Julies; her death was quick, but definitely not without pain.

Deb and her friend were deader than hell; they didn't know what hit them, and it was probably best that way. The beast couldn't take another victim shitting their pants today, and had she known what was happening, the whore would have definitely shit herself.

Chapter Seventeen

Kate had been kneeling outside what was left of her tent packing her belongings when she felt him. Kretha was calling to her! He was taunting her, and what he was showing her was horrific. She had been working hard to block her thoughts from Rooba and Red, but the disturbing images flashing through her mind were so powerful that she didn't even try to shut them out.

She sat back on her heels, closed her eyes, and let them come, sickened by what she saw, but allowing the disgust to fuel her rage. He would be able to sense her, if he for one moment thought that he had her, he would capitalize on it and come in for the kill.

Kate smiled grossly and chuckled as image after image invaded her.

An old man who she knew to be the Preacher, turned to Jell-O this morning. Next, was his taking of

Radka. He showed her how he strangled Jeff until he passed out, and then came the logging-truck driver. Both Jeff and Rad had been alive, but the driver opened fire and killed Rad. That is how Kretha became wounded and what had precipitated the war. She saw Rad's lifeless body, riddled with buckshot, falling to the ground and Jeff's body disintegrating as it flew into the windshield of the logging truck.

She heard the screams of the driver, and next she saw him hanging from one of the stakes attached to the trailer. Kate showed no emotion as she saw Kretha sitting next to a stream, still far from here. He'd come back to deliberately taunt her with a gift, he held up the mangled heads of two women with long, blond hair.

Both looked very similar to Kate, the woman were nearly unrecognizable, the fact that he held nothing but their heads was not lost on Kate. She struggled with the images but tipped her head back and laughed.

"Oh, you think you are so very wise, Chief Kretha, but you are a fool. Soon to be a very dead, hairy, ugly fool; both you and your Goya are going to rot in hell, Chief. Oh wait, you no longer have a Clan, so you are not a Chief any longer, are you? Oh, too bad about that, don't you think? Oh well. You know, I don't particularly like the name Kretha, and since I don't really like you either, I think I will simply call you "Stupid Mother Fucker." You know what that means don't you? It implies that not only are you dumb—foolish, in fact—but that you have bred your own mother. You, my friend, or shall I call you, my foe, are dead. I made you a promise this morning, and you did not listen. Do you know my name? I introduced myself to your son earlier. My name is Kate, and I am to be your killer. Enjoy your last hours because I am coming for you." Kate laughed maniacally before slamming her mind closed to him.

****

Rooba had stayed close to the female, and when Kretha had entered her mind, she had not been able to block him. Rooba had seen everything she had, and in turn, so had the Chief. Both Leviathans watched silently as the female waged an internal battle with the renegade of their own kind. They knew that they must not touch Kate's mind and offer support because to do so would tip Kretha off to their presence and it was important that he not know she had their support.

Rooba had told Khryl of Kate's plan to leave and possibly steal a Pain Stick and hunt them on her own. Khryl had already entered Kate's mind and had heard his and Kate's conversation. Khryl had alerted Merr-ee's sibling of her plan, and together they would keep her safe.

Rooba felt the moment Kate had closed her mind to the renegade. He prodded until she looked up. He nodded at her, encouraging her to let him in.

"Female, my Chief and I have seen what you have.

We are sorry for your pain and loss. You did well, female.

You must not allow him any control; he was trying to hurt

you and will continue to do so. Kretha must not know that

my Chief and I are here to help. We must exterminate the

renegade, and if he knows you are not alone, he will run.

Do you understand this, human?"

****

Kate was exhausted and pissed off. Joe had been

trying to talk to her, and she suspected that Rooba had

already sold her out. Dylan watched her like a hawk. Oh, he

knew what she had planned to do alright, and she was

going to hear about it eventually. Now fucking Rooba was

knocking at her mental door asking her if she got it.

"Umm, listen up, Rooba. I got it loud and clear,

and now can we get something clear between us? I call you

by your name each time I speak to you. I do not call you

Big Hairy Dumb Ass, I don't call you, Hey You Stinky Fuck, male, Bigfoot, Sasquatch, or anything other than Rooba, now do I? I'm guessing you heard what I call our new friend, and I don't want to have to come up with something similar for you. My name is Kate. If you call me female or human one more time, I am going to hurt you, do you understand me? I know you can call me Kate because you have done so, and I think you refer to me as human or female just to piss me off. It's working and I'm over it, so move on. I also know you sold me out to Dylan, and I don't appreciate him watching me." She paused.

"Now say, I am sorry for selling you out, Kate. I know you're smart." She turned to grin at the beast who just gaped at her in appalled horror. She heard Red snorting and assumed he had overheard.

****

Red decided that he had better say something on Rooba's behalf. He was indeed having a great time watching his warrior's interactions with Kate. Even though they were in the midst of tragedy again, he could not help but admire the grit of this female. He now understood why his Merr-ee liked Kate. Oh, how he wished Merr-ee could Mind Speak, but they got along just fine.

Kate was not being as kind to her mate as what Merr-ee was to Kooal, though, and he had wanted to talk to her about it. "Kate, you are a special human. Please do not become angry over my use of the word human. For many years my kind has only known your kind as man, male, female, or humans. Rooba does not mean to be rude. Sometimes I still refer to my Merr-ee as my human. I refer to Dylan as sibling of Merr-ee; it is how it is done. I must say that your choice of names for Kretha is bound to cause a stir. I like it, and I quite like having the ability to converse with you." Khryl nodded at her and continued. "I understand your pain, Kate, and hope you do not mistake our wish to help you as our way of taking over. That is not why we are here. We are here to help you, because you will need it, there are others here that wish to help you, too, and you are closing them out. Dylan has protected my Clan with his life, he fought alongside my warriors killing for you earlier. Your mate has come a long way to find you; he was here last year, Kate, and saw many ugly things, things man was never meant to see. I hope you can find it in your heart to forgive him because he was only doing what he thought was best. As Chief, I, too, have found myself doing what I thought was best, and it is with a heavy heart that I must admit the friend of Kooal was killed because I thought I knew best. You did a good job with the renegade, Kate, and Rooba is right: he can't know of us. I will say no more now." With that, he bowed his head to her and placed his hand over his heart.

****

Goya was ravaged with pain and confusion. Why had his father brought him to the camp under the presumption that they were going to scare the humans away? When they had arrived, Father had demanded that the humans be killed, and some of the warriors had wanted to refuse, as had Goya.

The Old Ones would surely be angry; the Gods would most certainly punish them to death! Father had insisted and said to go against his word meant death anyway. Father had not warned them of the Pain Sticks the humans carried or that the female had the ability to Mind Speak.

Some of the experienced warriors fought bravely, but Goya had no idea what to do. He was only fourteen summers in age and cowered in fear. The female with Mind Speak had known where he hid and used her Pain Stick. She had flung her fireballs at him, and they tore into his flesh, biting and stinging. His blood, dripping onto the leaves as the pain became almost unbearable. He had looked around for his father, he could not see him, and so he'd crawled away to the first shelter he could find.

He'd barely hidden himself when he'd heard the thunder and knew that warriors from another Clan had attacked and were killing his father's warriors. He still did not know where his father was. He just wanted to go home.

Goya rested but was woken up when the woman had again entered his head! She knew he was close and hurt. She knew his name and who his father was. She was going to hunt him if he did not stand down; he'd disobeyed the Law, and he knew what the punishment would be.

The female who had said her name was Kate had told him if he came to her, she would see he made it home to his mother and died honorably and was not destined to walk eternity in Hell, headless, no less. He felt the power of the woman and knew she spoke words of truth.

Goya loved his father, but his father had lied to him and the warriors. He had led them all to their deaths. Perhaps Goya could reason with the Mind Speaker. He was going to die one way or the other, but he wanted to do so in the arms of his mother.

He reached out to the woman with the power of the mind . . .

****

Kate was still reeling from her pseudo conversation with Red. She knew he was right and that Joe had done what he thought was right. Was it right? Hell, no. Did it completely destroy Kate for months? Yes, it did. But in the end, did she want to die on this mountain without thanking him for coming? She needed to at least do that much; things were happening so fast that Lord only knew what would happen next, and in the end, she knew she couldn't go home until it was done. She knew Joe wouldn't be here if it wasn't for her, and that meant something.

She made her way to where he sat at the fire. Dark was upon them, and they had built the fire up to epic proportions. She'd felt lucky an hour ago when the Forest Service had radioed that they were waiting for first light to come in and that the three survivors were safe. It gave her time to carry out her plan, but before she could do that, she had to do this.

"Hey, Joe," she said as she sat down beside him. "Sorry for punching you; I was just pissed, scared. No excuse, but I want you to know I appreciate you coming."

Joe had spent hours watching her, hardly believing she was still alive, and even more unbelievable was the fact that she could communicate with the beasts. He'd wanted to hug her and throw her over his shoulder and force her off the mountain, but he knew he'd fucked up six months ago, and that smart-ass Dylan had been right earlier after she'd decked him when he said to just sit back and shut his mouth. He'd said she'd come around.

He should have told her everything; they all should have told her. It killed him every week when he knew she left to come up here, and he would sit and drink himself to sleep each night until Cole called and told him she was safe or home.

How many times had he picked up the phone and dialed her number so he could explain it all to her, only to hang up before it ever rang? How many times had he driven all the way to Kalispell so he could sit her down and tell her the truth? If she wouldn't listen, then he knew Tom and Jace would. Hell, he knew Tom and Jace knew what was in these mountains! They'd even talked about it in an offhand manner. But nope, he couldn't stand up to Kate. Not headstrong and hell-bent Katie.

Now here he was, sitting around another damn fire, in the dark no less, with Dylan Fucking Thomas, waiting for a killer Bigfoot to attack. Christ. Some things never changed. He wanted to hug her, knowing how hard it must have been for her to come over and apologize, but he knew what she was planning to do, and there was not a chance in hell he was going to allow her to do it. He didn't have any idea yet what he was going to do. Maybe Dylan had handcuffs; God knew he had everything else. Joe couldn't be mad at the man sitting across the fire from him, though; he'd come when he'd called, and he hadn't asked questions.

"No worries, Kate, I deserved it. I'm glad you're okay."

"Uh, well, I'm still sorry. And thank you, I know that you probably would rather be anywhere but here." She made to rise, but he put his hand out to stop her.

"So what the hell is up with you communicating with them?" he said.

"I don't have any idea, Joe." She explained about hearing something the night before and then this morning just knowing. She said it was almost like she was in Joe's own head; she'd seen the body come flying out of the night. She seen Red leading Mari and Cole to safety, but she knew this one was different, and before she knew it, she was in his head and felt the evil. She shrugged and explained the headache. From there it was all downhill. When she'd returned from calling him and Mari this morning, she found that one of the campers had run off, and that was just the start. She told him about having just communicated with Kretha and that he'd killed two women. He'd taken their heads in the challenge that she'd thrown down.

She finally stopped and shuddered to think that she, in all likelihood caused the death of two more people. On the bright side, if there was one, her headache had gone away hours ago.

It was good to talk to Joe, just like old times. It was like nothing had changed, six months of anger had fallen away. She was wary of letting down her guard, though; Joe would never be on board with what was going to happen.

Joe looked at the woman he loved. She was still beautiful in all her rugged, dirty bitchiness. Even though one of his eyes was half swollen shut, and he could barely breathe through his nose that she'd broken, he still loved her and wasn't going to lose her.

If she was hell-bent on this fight, then he was going to do the only thing he could: he was going to fight it with her. What the hell did he have to lose? He'd already lost her. Maybe he could get her back.

"Katie." He said her name in a way that made her think they were in for a fight, but he surprised her. "I'm not going to try to talk you out of doing this because God knows I'd lose that fight and you. I'm not prepared to do either. What I am prepared to do is stand beside you. Tell me what you need from me, and I will do it."

Kate was speechless and nearly brought to tears; she wouldn't show it, but she was close to losing it. "Joe, I can't ask you to do that. I've seen into his head; he's coming back to kill me, Red and Rooba will help. I love you, Joe, and I can't have you dying because of me."

She looked at him and for the first time in her life felt whole and complete. They had been happy before, but it was this one moment of complete and total honesty that brought sunshine and clarity as it had never been before.

He laughed and hugged her. "None of us are going to die, Katie. I brought Dylan, remember?"

"Up yours, Roberts. I never said I was going to save your ass. I am here to kill me some ugly fucks, and as

I recall, you didn't bring me anywhere. I was here way before you," Dylan responded.

"Whatever man, you came and that's what counts." Joe smiled at Dylan.

Hell, Dylan thought, *shit was getting ugly and mushy up in here.* Damn Mari and her Bigfoot nonsense. At least he'd gotten to whack and stack a couple of the big bastards today. "Ah, go to hell, Joe," he replied. "Hey, how many rounds do you have for that piece of shit you're shooting? You need me to spot ya some?" Dylan laughed as he got up to do a sweep of the perimeter.

He couldn't stand anymore of the lovey-dovey bullshit, especially when he knew Kate intended to steal one of his guns the first chance she got. That Mind Speak crap might be good, but she wasn't able to hide everything, and Red had let him know she was planning to go rogue.

Chapter Eighteen

Kate was standing up to continue putting things in order when she felt the tugging in her mind. "Shit," she said. It was the young one. She didn't try hiding her thoughts from Red and Rooba. She was past the point of caring anyway, and what did it matter? It looked like they were all in this together. Or at least until she could distract them long enough to steal Dylan's automatic rifle and plenty of ammunition.

****

"Mind Speaker, can you hear me? It is I, son of Chief Kretha. I am known as Goya. I do not expect you to understand, but I wish to explain and if you still wish to honor me by returning me to my Clan for a proper burial, I will submit. I am dying anyway, abandoned by my father who was a liar and traitor to his Clan. Answer, Mind Speaker, do you hear my thoughts?"

****

"I hear you, Goya. I am Kate. Please continue, I will help you only as much as I can. You have sinned against my people. You know that. You know that even by the Laws of the Leviathans, your sins are punishable by death. But I will hear you." Kate looked at Red and Rooba. Both nodded at her to continue, indicating that they, too, could hear the young one.

****

"I am fourteen seasons old," he continued, his young voice catching on a sob. "I am wounded by your Pain Stick in many places, and my blood leaves my body; the pain is more than I can bear, and my father has abandoned me. I don't know where my mother is." He was openly weeping now. "I know not what day it is, only that the Gods have taken the sun. I fell asleep for awhile when the pain was less and have lost track of time. I'm hungry

and don't wish for you to take my head. I know that what happened was wrong, but I want to thank you for listening." He hiccupped before continuing.

"It was afternoon when my father came to the Clan; he was enraged and covered in blood. He said that the warriors must gather immediately, and I was to join in as we were going to scare some humans away from our valley. He said that you were bad humans and had brought death with you. He urged us to hurry so that we could have you gone before nightfall. When we got to your camp, we saw that the humans were sitting around much the same as you always had done when you came to this valley. We have watched you many times. This time, however, my father said that we must kill you all. Some of the warriors tried to rebel and said that the Gods would punish them with death. Father said that if they did not kill everyone in the human camp, he would kill them, including me. I had never even gone on a hunting party before; we only eat berries and

fish, and I knew not what to do, so I hid. My father screamed and threw a boulder into your camp. I saw it hit the man, breaking his leg. The other warriors yelled, but they hesitated to harm you. Father tore a tree from the earth and hit one of the warriors with it; he told the others this would be their fate if they did not fight."

Goya paused; he could feel himself slipping into darkness

"When you started using your Pain Sticks, the warriors were wounded by the fireballs, and Father became enraged. He pulled me from my hiding place and threw me down the hill. It was then that I was wounded by many of the stinging fireballs. I pretended I was dead, and I watched as Father ran to one of your Noise Makers and threw it on the man. He then ran away, left his warriors and me to fight alone, to die alone. I heard the thunder and knew that warriors from another Clan had arrived, so I crawled to this cave where I now lie." He sobbed. "I ask

your forgiveness, Mind Speaker, for harming your people. I did not know what I was taking part in, but that is no excuse. I am a Leviathan and the heir of a Chief. I know the Laws. I don't think I can come to you but do not wish to anger you. I do not want you to take my head, and I don't wish to walk eternity in Hell with my father. Please take my life, and then allow me to go home to my mother. I beg you to end my torment. That is all I can ask. I will lead you to where I now shelter." Goya sobbed as pain filled his young body.

****

Kate had fallen to her knees, tears streaming down her face as she listened to the young one's story. She could see into his mind and knew his words were the truth. She did not need him to lead her to where he hid; she already knew. She also knew that she would not kill the cub but turn him over to Khryl to do with what he saw fit.

The young one had no choice, and he knew not what he was being forced to do. None of the warriors did. Kate knew that Kretha would be listening, however, and that she must remain strong. He must think that she had killed his son, or she would never have her chance at him.

She looked up at Khryl, and he nodded his approval as did Rooba. Kate had no idea that Joe was by her side or that Dylan had covered their backs during the time she was down. She stood slowly and drew in a deep breath. "I accept your apology, Goya. I will honor your warrior's spirit and allow you to return to your mother in death so that your remains may be returned to the earth and your spirit can walk with the Gods. Guide me to your shelter."

****

"Thank you, Mind Speaker. Follow my thoughts up the mountain. I am not far. I am hidden just inside the cave

that faces the valley. I can see the glow from your fire. I have no weapon; I give myself to you freely.

****

Rooba was sprinting up the mountain in a matter of seconds. The young one would not be killed. Kate and the Chief had said so, but it was his duty to retrieve the wounded cub. He was the quickest, and this way Kretha would have no way of hearing Kate's thoughts. Rooba blocked his thoughts the entire run; Kretha must not know Kate had help from him or Khryl.

When he entered the cave, he was to raise his mighty fist and knock the cub unconscious as quickly as possible. Goya would think that death was coming for him and his father would feel it.

They hoped that Kretha would believe Kate had betrayed Goya and taken his head, driving the renegade mad. By the time Goya woke up, he would be too far away for Kretha to read his thoughts and know any different.

Cro and Zon were returning, and one of them would take the cub to his mother where he would be closely guarded until it was made certain he did not have any of his father's tendencies, even then it would be up to Khryl if the cub lived.

Khryl had instructed Kate to enter the forest and project to Kretha that she was going for his heir and that she was coming for him next. She was closely guarded, of course, but Kate did not need the Pain Sticks the other humans carried; she had the power to know what her adversary was thinking, and the closer he got, she was able to feel where the renegade hid.

Rooba was approaching the cave's entrance and could hear the pitiful moans from inside. He quickly scented the air checking for any signs of danger. He smelled only the young one who was expiring quickly if the additional smell of infection was any indication.

He rushed inside the darkness, his eyes needing no time to adjust, and upon seeing the young Leviathan, struck him in the head before the cub even had a chance to open his eyes and register that it was not the Mind Speaker who had come for him. He picked up the frail cub, instantly angry that any father would take such a young one, the heir to the Clan, no less, into battle. Rooba did not have a mate yet, so he did not have cubs, but the dignity and honor that this little one had, when he'd called out to Kate and asked for a swift death was impressive. He hoped that if he ever had cubs of his own, he would be a better father and never put his son into a position where he had to beg for his death.

Rooba exited the cave and sped down the mountain. The young one did not have much time. They would need to help him and keep his presence a secret from Kretha before one of the others took him across the mountains, or he would surely die.

"Chief, I have the cub; he is gravely ill. I fear he will not survive the journey if we do not do something to help him first. Kate needs to keep telling Kretha that he is dead. I am coming as fast as I can."

****

"I will instruct Kate but she is doing fine on her own. Bring the boy to me. I will use some of the humans' medicines on him myself if I have to. I have already called to Cro and Zon. They will be here soon, and I will send them both back with him. Hurry, Rooba, there is no time; Kretha is angry."

****

"How does it feel, you slimy bastard? Or should I say, you Mother Fucker? Goya is dead; I've taken your precious heir's life. Do you feel it? Do you feel the emptiness inside you knowing that your son is dead? That I, a mere female, a human no less, has taken your heirs pathetic, little life. It was easy you know; he begged me to come for him. He lay there and let me snuff out his life. I bet you thought I would care about that little impromptu share session you gave me earlier. You have forgotten one thing, oh mighty fallen Chief: I am the ruler of your world now, and nothing you can do bothers me. Did you really think a few dead bodies and two severed heads were going to scare me? What, did you think that I was going to run away? I promised that I would kill you, and I never break a promise. I gave you a chance, and you pissed it away. After all these years of watching me, and I knew you watched me, I could feel you! I thought you would have known me better. I am coming for you next. Don't close your eyes, mighty one, because you will not hear me coming for you. I know you are wounded as well, and perhaps you will beg me to take your life just as your precious Goya did. I am undecided, though, as I sit here staring at his lifeless body: should I keep my word and return his body to the Clan, or should I instead take his head? I guess you will find out, won't you?"

With that, Kate slammed her mind shut. She could feel Kretha's rage, and she knew Rooba would be returning soon with Goya. She was too exhausted to allow him in even for a second and had kept up a steady projection of evil and hate to goad him the way Khryl had said to. There was no doubt in her mind that it was enough. He wasn't close, but Kate had no problem picking up his approximate location. She vowed to keep that detail to herself.

Chapter Nineteen

Kate was just exiting the forest when Rooba ran back into camp holding the lifeless form of the cub. He was surprisingly small for fourteen summers; Kate had assumed he would be large like Red and Rooba.

She hurried to the fire where Rooba laid the young Leviathan. He was perhaps a little over five feet tall, maybe 120 pounds. Not really much different than your average fourteen year old, except he was covered in hair and had the features she had come to expect from that of a Bigfoot.

His body was riddled with buckshot that she knew to be hers and felt immediate guilt. No one else within her camp carried a shotgun but her.

Kate had spent a lot of summers patching up people and had even stitched up a couple. The medical kit was in fairly decent shape, and she set to work cleaning him up. He couldn't be allowed to wake, so she gave him a mild sedative that would also help with some of his pain along with an antibiotic shot.

She wasted no time pouring peroxide straight onto the wounds that had already begun to fester and ooze yellow pus thanks to the lead shot lodged in his slight body.

With Joe at her side, she used light from the fire to probe each tiny hole and extract the small ball of lead. When she was sure she had them all, she cleaned each wound again and put antibiotic salve on them. Kate had estimated that Goya had taken two rounds from her shotgun.

She'd pulled a total of twelve balls of lead from his body, and she knew her gun was loaded with 6 shot. It was a wonder that she hadn't cut him in two; the only thing that saved his life was that he was grossly out of range for the shotgun. It did little to ease her guilt, but she had to harden herself with the knowledge that she did not know, and she was protecting the lives of many. Kate loaded two more syringes with sedative and antibiotic and told Khryl to have his warriors give them to Mari or Cole. She would call with instructions, but he would need them soon after they got him over the mountains. The rest was up to Mother Nature and whatever natural remedies the Clan had.

As Cro and Zon took the boy and began their journey with him across the mountains, Khryl was sure to warn them to guard their thoughts. Kretha would be plotting an attack, and they had no way of knowing where or when unless Kate could feel him. If he chose to attack Khryls Clan, they would be helpless. This was a constant worry for her; she knew that both Mari and Cole were very close to the Clan as well. Kretha would have no problems killing two humans if he knew they were important to her.

Kate checked her watch and was astonished to find that it was only ten o'clock. She would have guessed it was much later; she'd been going strong since the night before.

To relax now was to commit suicide. As much as she didn't want to do it, she needed to crack open the vault that was her mind and see what Kretha was up to.

She sat down with Joe at the fire and reached for his hand while closing her eyes. She was immediately assaulted by the violent images Kretha was spewing. She saw her own face as he saw it and was shocked by his evil.

He had ravaged her face until nothing was left; the fact that she could recognize herself was a feat unto itself. She forced herself to giggle knowing he could feel her.

"Ah, such violence and rage, your efforts are wasted, oh fallen one." She immediately closed the door before she could see or feel anything else.

****

Dylan Thomas was getting impatient; he didn't like sitting around with his thumbs in his ass. If something needed killing then, dammit, let him get to it. He had a family to get back to and as much as he enjoyed his job, he wasn't getting paid for this shit.

He studied the other two humans with him. Kate Mitchell was pretty badass; he would give credit where credit was due, and she had proven that she could hold her own. She reminded him of Mari; both of them walked around these mountains with a 12 gauge and a chip on their shoulders. It was kind of cool, he admired a woman with grit, and he had no damned time for a pussyfooted, bawl-baby bitch of a woman.

Where Mari intended to save every damned Bigfoot she found, he had no doubt in his mind that if provoked, Kate would level the species, if for no other reason than to get the bastards out of her head. He didn't envy her that little problem. It would be nice to be able to communicate with Red and his Clan, but he suspected she'd been privy to some pretty ugly shit spewed her way by Kretha, the

"Mother Fucker," as Kate called him. At least the lady could string together a few swear words that made him smile.

Dylan knew Joe Roberts was a good guy; this wasn't the first time they had sat around a campfire waiting for a deranged, serial-killing Bigfoot to come their way, and just like before, he was a pretty calm guy. Joe was the complete opposite of his brother, Jack, who was Dylan's sister, Mari's, father-in-law.

Jack was a no-nonsense sonofabitch, and Dylan liked the hell out of him. Jack and Dylan's dad, Matt, had become good friends. These days they spent most of their time over on the Thompson seeing which one could out fly fish the other.

Joe was more like his nephew, Cole. Dylan's brother-in-law was a pretty cool cat under pressure and had survived five days alone last September while being hunted by a rogue Bigfoot. He'd finally found Mari at the fire tower on Richards Peak, but with a fire raging down their throats, they'd been forced to run right into the belly of the beast. Luckily, that was where Red had come in. The giant red Bigfoot was the Chief of his Clan and literally a gentle giant. Dylan knew that Red loved his sister and she him. He knew had it not been for Red, they would have lost both Mari and Cole to the killer last year, he hoped like hell that the old beast had it in him to go another round.

Last year he'd had his dad, Joe, Jack, Maggie Roberts, Silas Baldwin, and a man named Bill—who had unfortunately been killed—alongside him. They'd been armed to the teeth and had full-size trucks for protection if needed. Tonight he had Joe Roberts, Kate Mitchell, and two Bigfoot. Granted these two Bigfoot were large, badass, hairy fuckers, but they didn't pack the fire power Dylan liked.

He took stock of what he had to work with; of course, he had The Big Gun, a Weatherby, 30-378 with a precision scope dialed in to shoot the balls off a gnat's ass. Granted it didn't hold a lot of rounds, but it usually only took one to get the job done. Extra ammo was never an issue with him anyway.

He knew from prior experience that the Weatherby would knock the asshole right out of one of these shit heads. Dylan checked the AR-10 that was strapped to his chest; it was calibrated in 308 and there were four 30-round magazines attached to his combat vest as well. He'd modified the trigger group and turned the semi-automatic into full auto after last year's little fiasco.

Luckily, he was a big man and could carry all this shit because rounding out his arsenal was a 460 Smith and Wesson Revolver; she was a real beauty, and he'd spared no expense when he'd bought the extra 5-shot speed loaders. He also carried a large hand-honed knife that Silas

Baldwin had given him last year; it would cut through a spinal cord like butter. Everything combined with the weight of his pack that never left his back was upwards of fifty pounds, and he was damned proud that he was fit enough to carry it and never flinch.

All he would need was one second to line the shot up and let it go. He wouldn't waste time lining up a head shot, but instead go for the kill, the chest being a bigger target, and one round to the heart was fatal. It also gave him time to double tap the bastard if need be.

He would have to be careful that Red and Rooba stayed out of his shooting lane. And he would need to know what Kate and Joe had for backup firepower. He knew Kate had a 12 gauge shotgun and a .45, but she'd been engaged in a firefight earlier, and her situation on ammo was questionable. He had a pretty good idea what Joe carried; he remembered last year when he'd posed the exact same question, and it felt like a bad fucking dream instead of déjà vu'.

"Hey, love birds, hate to break up the reunion, but it's that time again, when I ask you what you're packing for firepower and ammo. Kate, I know you had intended to go this alone or steal one of my guns, but the jig is up; how much ammo do you have left for the shotgun and that .45?"

"Uh, not nearly enough, Dylan. The shotgun is loaded; Mari removed the plug from the tube, so I've got a total of seven, its buckshot number 6, with rotating slugs. I have one magazine with nine rounds for the .45. I found Blake's and Rich's guns, but both were empty, and I've gone through their tent and packs looking for extra ammo, and there was none. I guess they didn't think they would need it, or they used it during the attack. I used two boxes of shotgun shells myself." She shrugged, "It's all I've got."

"What about you, Joe?" Dylan asked. He hoped that Joe had come prepared. He'd been around a time or two and knew what to expect; in fact, Dylan knew that Joe should be more than prepared.

"AR-15 in 223, four 30-round aftermarket magazines with 77 grain SMK-HPs, I'm full auto, but I guess you know that already, don't ya, Dylan, since this is your setup?" The men shared a grin. "I might have a couple other things as well, depends on the situation. I have a few containers of Sure Shot. I suppose, strategically placed, we might be able to blow something's head off." Joe looked damned pleased with himself.

"Nice, Joe, I approve. I have a few containers of it myself. We can talk about how to use it if the need arises. I see you still have the 460 Smith. Have you been practicing?"

"I'll never be up to your standards, Dylan, but I'm good to go," Joe smirked.

Kate chimed in, "Wow, boys, why don't you both just whip 'em out and measure? See who's got the bigger piece. You two look like children for Christ's sake."

Dylan grinned at her and stood up. "Well, I'm game. How 'bout you, Joe? You wanna whip it out so your girlfriend can see which one of us is the bigger . . . uh . . . child?" He snorted with laughter as he walked away. Had to give her credit, she was a real bitch.

Chapter Twenty

Kretha was in a full-blown rage. His only son was dead! The little, simpering coward had given himself up to the female. He'd given away his life to a human, a female no less. The idea was mind-numbing. Goya deserved to walk for eternity, headless, within the scorching heat that was hell! What had he been thinking? Kretha had heard every word Goya told the Mind Speaker who called herself Kate. His son, his heir, had told the human his secrets. Had told of his betrayal to his warriors! He knew Goya had been wounded, but he would have gone back and saved his only son.

Was this the emotion that many called grief? He cared not that his mate and daughter had taken refuge within the shelter of the other Clan. If anything, it confirmed what he had known all along: they were mindless, pathetic females that belonged to a Clan that was not worthy of the Leviathan name. One day he would find his mate and other child, and perhaps he would kill them both. The truth was he simply did not care about them and never had. Their betrayal nagged at the corners of his conscience, he was wounded, hungry, and exhausted. What he felt toward them in anger was nothing compared to the rage he felt toward Goya and the Mind Speaker.

His son, dead and disgraced at the hands of another human, his heart burned with the need to seek revenge. Kretha would make the human female and all those that followed her into his wilderness pay for their act of violence.

They had disrespected his kind by coming here in the first place. Had he and his warriors not spent many precious hours watching them? Had he not allowed the female with the yellow hair to come into his home for many seasons?

Kretha was a Chief and even though he knew many in his Clan feared him, he had always been honorable and seen to it they had plenty of food and had never suffered needlessly at the hands of man. When the humans and their Noise Makers came, he had withdrawn into the forest, deeper into the cold and inhospitable mountains where food was often a challenge to obtain. He had silently gone hungry so that the Old Ones and the rest of the Clan could eat. Kretha had never complained even though it angered him that a great Chief should have his needs put below those that were dead and dying.

Kretha consoled himself with the fact that he had influenced many generations, his warriors, though few, had gone into battle and died with honor in his stead. He thought back to the exact moment when he had seen Goya hiding.

He was angry that he and his warriors, who had fought many a battle with other Clans and wild animals, had been cut down with the Pain Sticks. Even more angered that the other Clan had ravaged what was left of their already wounded and dying bodies.

Kretha knew the other Clan would bury the giants within the forest. They would be sure to hide the evidence of the bodies and battle, but it did not rest lightly with Kretha that so many warriors had been put in the ground without the proper rituals. This could not be allowed. He convinced himself that for that atrocity alone, the humans would pay. He refused to acknowledge his misdirection and lies that led to their death in the first place.

It was a Chief's right to direct his warriors where they were best suited to protect the Clan. He had, in fact, told them many untruths and forced them into battle, but his intentions, he believed, were honorable, and for that, the humans would die. As their Chief, it would be up to him to right the wrong of those who died in the forest.

He would rest and then pursue his new mission. He was no longer a great and honorable Chief; he was a killer and a man-hunter that would take the life of at least one more human before he ran and hid like a coward to plot his next revenge.

Chapter Twenty-One

Dylan did a quick perimeter check and found, to his surprise, that all was clear, and the sounds of nature had returned. Even with the birds chirping and other creatures chattering, Dylan knew it was only a matter of time before shit hit the fan.

Khryl and Rooba had alternately taken positions guarding the camp, but dark was fully upon them. Dylan knew what the dark brought. This wasn't his first rodeo with the beasts, nor was it his first go-round in the bowels of hell. Through his life he had seen and endured a lot, but it made him what he was, and he believed that he was a tough son-of-a-bitch.

Dylan watched Kate and Joe quietly from his side of the fire. He was glad that they had worked their shit out, but he didn't trust Kate. She had a plan and didn't see fit to make him or Joe privy to what it was. Dylan was not above using Red for information; sometimes it paid to have a sister that thought Bigfoot was her long-lost buddy. Red, in turn, did his job of protecting what he thought Mari held dear, and Dylan and Kate were two things Mari loved. He had to admit, if he could get over how damn ugly they were and the stench that followed them everywhere, the beasts were cool. He had, for once, taken a break in his career and rejoiced in his unofficial capacity of Sasquatch Security.

Joe's chuckle had him raising his head. He really didn't care what the lovebirds chatted about, but what he did care about was Kate's life, and he suspected that at this point she had little in the way of regard for it herself. He doubted he would fall asleep, but again having two giant beasts around to work the perimeter had its merits, and he could use a little rest. He knew, though, that the minute he or Joe turned his back on her, she would be gone.

She acted innocent and appeared to be content with the way things were playing out, but his gut told him different. Oh no, Kate Mitchell was not only a great business woman, she was a bitch and a force to be reckoned with. At that moment, Dylan decided that rather than stay awake all night and put himself at risk, he was going to tell her a thing or two about guns, pursuing the enemy, and how to win a battle. Joe would be pissed, but it wasn't in Dylan's nature to beat around the bush. She needed to know because Kate's newfound communicating skills were badass and likely to take her far, but when it came to brute strength, she didn't hold a candle to these big bastards.

Clearing his throat, he looked directly at her across the fire. He would be discreet for Joe's sake, but even though Kate could now communicate with the Leviathans, he thought she was smart enough to understand every word he was about to say, or rather, the ones he didn't say.

"So I guess we can assume that the hairy shit is going to do what they all do, wait until dawn to attack." He paused and glared at Kate; she held his stare. "Joe is outfitted damn well if I do say so myself, and there is no doubt in my mind that his AR can take down this bastard." He nodded at Joe but again looked at Kate and narrowed his eyes.

"Joe, back when you were getting set up, we really never had a chance to talk about shit outside of what the rifle could do. For example, it is not a light weight gun, and if you have to pack it for awhile, the best way to do it is to use your tactical sling. Let your body absorb the weight of the weapon. When you get into position, where it's time to fire, and I know you're a good hunter, but when it is life or death, all types of shit are gonna flood your mind." Dylan paused.

"Put it all aside, focus on your target. Control your breathing, become one with your gun, the surroundings, even what you're about to take out."

Joe was nodding his head, and Kate had sat up straight and stared intently at Dylan. He knew that she was picking up what he was laying down. Her intent was clear, and he would do his damned to have her back, but Dylan didn't think Kate wanted backup; this was personal, and he knew about personal. However, making the fight too personal would dull her senses and the natural skill she possessed.

"When you know the enemy is near, you need to take shelter, find a shooting lane, and listen. Nature is going to tell you what is happening, but it is up to you to listen. Covering your scent is the hardest thing when you're tracking an animal; I have some elk piss that is going to work for that, and you need to use it. The most important thing is that when you acquire your target; do not let your emotions cloud what you have come to do."

Dylan glanced up from the fire, looking to where Kate and Joe sat.

"You won't have time to think about it. Raise your gun, lean into the shot, and let the round go. I don't care what you have been told about breathing and holding your breath. It's all going to come to you, *if* you're in the killing zone. Whatever you do don't jerk the trigger, hell, to be honest, I no longer think about squeezing it. I just let instinct take control. Once you've acquired the target, remain calm, but always remember, shit has gotten real. This is when you simply let the shot go; own the bastard's ass, always assume that he or it is not alone. Where there is one, there is likely to be more."

Dylan paused to make sure they were both listening. He'd definitely captured his audience. Good he thought, God willing they would survive, however shit ran downhill and Dylan wasn't a betting man. The odds were sketchy at best.

"And for God's sake, do not ever assume that one shot is enough. I don't care if you have to double tap the big asshole or empty your entire magazine into its head, make sure that it is dead. Do you both understand what I am saying?"

He watched them closely. Joe would risk his life to follow Kate; to that end, Dylan had absolutely no doubt. Kate, on the other hand, had no intentions of ever letting that happen.

She was focused; the sparks shooting from her eyes and smirk on her face proved to him that she was more than a little dangerous. Christ, he hoped to hell she wasn't suicidal as well. He stared at her for a moment and nodded his head. A brief glance at Joe momentarily caught Dylan unaware. The man was watching her as well. Love might blind a man, but he couldn't help but grin; these Roberts men weren't as dumb as they looked. Okay, maybe that was a harsh assumption, but he'd seen the man Joe was a year ago become a withering shell when Kate had left him.

He grinned to himself. Ole Joe might not be as aware of what Kate had up her sleeve, but he wasn't a fool.

****

Kate stared back at Dylan Thomas, putting the emptiest look on her face that she possessed, but she was shrewd. There was little doubt in her mind that Mari's brother knew exactly what she planned. Even had she not read Red's thoughts and knew he had informed the strange man of what she planned to do, she was positive that Dylan would have known.

Joe was a little easier to manipulate, and she knew that it would be his gun she took. Dylan had made eye contact with her and then looked directly at the rifle that sat between her and Joe.

Dylan would never allow her to get close enough to steal his gun. Joe's however was within reach, even though he would be pissed and a little hurt, she had no qualms about reminding him that when this was over, he owed her.

Kate grinned, realizing that she was already one step ahead by planning to win this; Dylan would advise her to not get cocky, and she wouldn't, but she was going home. Kate had no idea when that might be, but she had already filled her pack with what little food and water she had. She'd scavenged a blade from Richard's body, and before he had left, Ben had quietly slipped her, his and Mimi's extra ammo. All together it amounted to quite a few rounds that neither Joe nor Dylan knew she had.

When the time came, she had also pilfered the extra ammo out of Blake's tent. Kate knew she had lied to the men about her situation regarding ammo, but what they didn't know wouldn't hurt them. It was fortunate that Blake had purchased the exact same pistol just days after Kate had bought hers, all the extra ammo might come in handy.

There was no such thing as too much firepower when you went to war. She also intended to make use of Dylan Thomas's ATV. Earlier, she had noticed some sort of pack, and she had given it a feel up. She had no doubt that at his handy disposal, was the equivalent of a Montanan's version of a Militia bag. She'd be taking it.

It was way past dark, and the midnight hour was approaching. She'd hoped that both men would tire out, and she could quietly slip away.

The beasts they called friends wouldn't be as easily fooled, but Dylan had opened himself up when he'd told her about the elk piss he intended to use. If she could get to it, so be it. If not, she would use every last brain cell she had to find the bastard. If uglies one and two followed, which she suspected number two, Rooba, would definitely do, then there was nothing she could do about it. She would not hurt him as there was not a doubt in her head that she'd be dead if not for Red.

Kate acknowledged the debt she owed Mari's Red, and would see that it was repaid. Killing his sidekick wasn't exactly conducive to making friends with the local Bigfoot population. Besides, she was determined and stubborn, but she wasn't a damn idiot; the big "know-it-all" could prove he was useful.

Kate pretended to stretch and yawn. There was no way this was going to be easy, so she might as well call a spade a spade. Joe had no idea what she was planning, and there was only so much she could get away with from Dylan; she knew that no matter what she did, he was going to pursue her, and that was fine. More than anything, though, she didn't want Mari's brother to get hurt; he had a family that she liked very much. His death would not be on her shoulders.

Another plan was forming in her mind. She felt almost as evil and diabolical as the beast she knew to be just out of her range of communications. Kate was going to go to the bathroom and snatch Dylan's bag, her pack that was hidden just out of sight.

When she came back from her nonexistent bathroom trip, she was going to make her run. The two men and the beasties would be pissed. Joe was going to be shocked; she'd use that shock to hold him at gunpoint and steal his rifle. All the while, she had to block those images from her head and throw out ridiculously stupid ones in their place.

Red and Rooba were going to get a head full of womanly love; maybe she'd even put some images out there about her wedding and make it as sappy and pathetic as she could handle. Hopefully, they would tune her out. When she was a safe distance away, she would let them know to help Joe and Dylan.

No matter what, Kate didn't want any of them hurt. If there was time, she would knock them out and tie them up, but she had a hunt to get to. The best thing to do was throw Dylan off and hope like hell he didn't need to go back to his ATV for anything. She was going to just come out and ask for the elk piss.

Chapter Twenty-Two

"So, Dylan, let's have that elk pee. No point in getting caught with our pants down." She dared him to deny her request. To do so would put Joe on alert and neither one wanted that. He stared at her for a brief second and without breaking eye contact with her, tossed the bottle across the fire. When she caught it with one hand, his eyes narrowed on her shrewdly.

She merely nodded and stood up. "I'm going to find a bush that has my name on it. No peeking." She said to no one in particular, but her gaze traveled to Joe. Kate smiled at him; he'd come for her in her time of need. She loved him and hoped what was about to happen wouldn't ruin what they'd rekindled. She'd spent months without him and could do so again if need be.

She looked at Dylan across the fire. It was casting shadows on his face, but she had no doubt he watched her.

She let her spine stiffen and the emotion fall from her face as she looked at him. She smiled and nodded to him, but before she walked away, she saw him stiffen in response. Kate didn't miss his smirk or the challenge in his eyes.

****

Dylan watched Kate walk away from the circle of firelight. He wouldn't misjudge the woman again. He stood and looked around. Joe watched her as well, and Dylan struggled with himself on whether or not he should tell the man what was about to happen.

He caught movement and immediately knew it was Red. The beast had watched Kate walk away, had it not been for Red, Dylan would have suspected what she planned, but would not have guessed the lengths she was going to go to achieve it. Even now he was unsure.

Joe's rifle rested next to him as it had all night; surely, she wouldn't go off without it. He hoped that Red and Rooba kept an eye on her.

He was about to blow her cover with Joe, and he knew the man wasn't going to handle the news very well.

"So, Joe, you do realize that Kate intends to steal your rifle and go after the hairy bastard on her own, right?" Again he knew he lacked a filter but wasn't honesty best? What the hell?

"Ah, Dylan, I'm not stupid. I lived with the woman for years. I never know what the hell is going through her head, but I do know that Katie has a plan, I'm guessing that you know what it is?" He chuckled and smiled at Dylan before continuing. "So, did ole' Red read her mind and fill you in on the diabolical workings of Kate Mitchell's mind? If he did, tell him to try and figure out where the hell I stand with her because I might just be tired and on edge, but I would imagine that Kate is about to cause a shit storm, real soon. To be honest, I would like to know if I am still in the shitter before I die."

Dylan looked at Joe for a second and had to admit that he'd misjudged him, again. He would never have called Joe stupid, but he would have bet his last dollar that when it came to Kate, he was a lovesick, blind fool. He laughed.

This was going to get fucking ugly, of that he had no doubt. Ugly always meant a damned mess, but it usually meant a little fun in the process. What the hell? He was already here, might just as well get 'er done.

"Red indicated she was going to swipe one of the rifles and go walkabout. You might as well just hand her the gun, Joe; it's gonna save us time in the long run, and you can plan to eat shit if you want, but I'm going home. Alive."

"What do you think she has planned?" Joe asked, cautiously looking around him. Today was almost too easy, and that raised red flags. It wasn't just the ease of rescuing Kate and the campers, but Kate was being nice. With Katie, that could only mean trouble. She was being particularly nice to him. He'd give it twenty more minutes. Nothing was ever easy, and she was never docile. It wouldn't last.

"Well, I imagine she is going to walk in here and do something fucking nasty and steal your gun. Kate's got balls, but she wouldn't try to take my rifle." Dylan smirked. "You ever heard of the Bait and Switch, Joe?" Joe nodded and shrugged. "Well, I say we just sit back and close our eyes. She's gonna walk in here, and whatever nasty, bitchy shit she has planned will be of no use to her. Wait until she attempts to play her hand and take her out."

"Take her out? Christ, what does that even mean, Dylan?"

"It means that she isn't going anywhere, least of all alone. I'm all in, but I won't have her death on my conscience. Face it, you know I don't give two fucks 'bout you, buddy, but I just don't need the hassle of pissing my sister off." Dylan leaned back and closed his eyes.

****

Shit! She was really sick and tired of men. Kate glared at the two of them sitting around the campfire. It was bad enough that the arrogant son-of-a-bitch, Dylan, knew her plan. Oh well, she'd make a couple adjustments and be golden. Did he think she was stupid? She had circled camp listening to their conversation.

Kudos, Joe, she thought. Kate was beginning to wonder if the silent man was ever going to stand up to her.

It didn't matter, though; she wouldn't be stopped. Momentarily detoured, but just as Mr. Big Gun over there didn't want her death on his conscience, she didn't want either of theirs on hers. So if it was hardball he wanted it was hardball she would give them.

She looked over to where the two hairy assholes stood in the trees. She didn't have to see them to know where they were. It still kind of freaked her out, but something in her had snapped this morning. Kate didn't have time to try and figure out what the hell was wrong with her brain, at least not yet.

"Red." She thought his name, and at once, she was in. "I'm not going to hurt either of them, but I think we can agree that it would be best if they dropped out of the hunt. If you attack me, I swear that I will never stop searching and if it means war, then so be it. I am asking you to protect Joe and Mari's brother. This can't ever end well; something or someone is going to die. You owe Mari, do you not? I owe you, and my repayment will be keeping my silence of your existence. You are nothing but an overly large bear."

She looked at the eyes that had begun to glow from just inside the forest.

What the hell was he doing? Kate could feel the tension radiating off Rooba and decided he, too, needed a lecture. She rolled her shoulders and shifted her eyes.

"Oh, Rooba, my friend, there's no need to get your fur in a twist." She smiled. "I told you already that you could come along and play, but let's not forget by whose rules. I've got one dickhead like you to kill; please don't make me have to explain this all again. It makes my head hurt, and that pisses me off. Do you know what it means to piss off a woman?"

As Kate spoke, she dropped her pants behind Dylan's ATV. As she fiddled casually with what she hoped looked like the real deal of her peeing, she reached up and snagged the tactical bag off the hook Dylan had attached near the handle bars. To Kate's delight, it was a fanny pack of some sort that she could tie around her waist. Once she was back at the fire, the men would be none the wiser for her theft.

She only had a second to peak into it but knew it contained Sure Shot, a flashlight; an extra magazine for what she could only hope was the .45 that he didn't tell anyone about, and an extra knife. A few odds and ends like rope and some snacks—not too bad of a haul.

It was going to be a good day for killing. Thank, you, Dylan Asshole Thomas.

****

Khryl had carefully observed this human Mind Speaker. He had been mindful to guard his thoughts from her as had Rooba. It made it hard for him to communicate with his warrior, and Khryl found himself agitated.

Merr-ee's human was impetuous but acted with the heart of a true hunter.

Khryl didn't know how she spoke to his kind, at first he was startled and put on guard. Her body spoke the same words as her head, and he, Khryl, believed the human to be special. She had blocked him from her thoughts for several hours, but he'd watched her body tense with each passing minute. It was time.

Khryl had done nothing as she had spoken within his mind; he'd listened, and when she stopped, he had been powerless against her will. He snorted as he realized that she was not affected by his gaze. The human sneered at him, and he could think of no other emotion but disdain to describe what she was feeling in that moment. Khryl had thought of many ideas to stop her and hunt the renegade himself, but in the end, there was nothing he could do.

Khryl could tell Rooba was annoyed. His agitation was clear for all to see, but hurting the female would anger Merr-ee's sibling, and the large human male was part of his Clan. The male was a warrior and would be treated with the same respect due to any Leviathan protecting his Chief.

Khryl was the Chief and even though he did not understand how this female communicated with her mind, he would not tolerate her disrespect. Rooba was barely containing his anger; Khryl would need to put an end to this at once.

"I hear your words, female. I caution you to act with the heart of the warrior I know to beat within your chest. Rooba and I are not your enemies your ability to use Mind Speak is curious. I respect the warrior's soul you have, but your insolence will not be tolerated. I am the Chief of my Clan, friend to Merr-ee and Kooal, and have come not because they asked, but to exterminate the

renegade that hides within these woods. A great injustice

has been done to you and your kind, my heart is filled with

sorrow for your loss, but you are of no match for the

Leviathan that is called Kretha. I will protect your Joe and

the sibling of Merr-ee, but I shall protect you, too. I mean

you no disrespect; you will hunt beside us, with us."

Khryl saw the fire behind her eyes and could hear

her heartbeat begin to race; oh yes, this female was angry.

"You will not disrespect me or my warrior again, Kate."

Khryl flashed his gaze to the men at the fire and realized he

had emerged from the shadows during the confrontation.

He took a deliberate step away allowing the darkness to

shield him once again.

He had spoken his piece and would now observe

her in silence.

Chapter Twenty-Three

Kate's anger was palpable. She had to breathe deeply and focus to control the rage that built within her while remaining careful that the wall to her mind was firmly in place. So, he thought she had the heart of a warrior, did he? He thought that he called the shots and she would just buckle to his will. She grinned as she continued to stare at the trees where he had disappeared. Kate had no doubt that he continued to watch her for a reaction. She had felt his annoyance when that "look into my eyes" bullshit hadn't worked and had felt the tension from Rooba as well.

There was no way in hell she was going to give either of them the satisfaction of an outburst. During Red's speech, Kate had deliberately ignored Rooba's presence. No point in making him think she gave a shit. In fact, she was nearing a point where she didn't care what they did as long as they stayed out of her way.

Red wasn't going to take the bait and bow to her will either. She'd feel momentarily shitty if Mari's pets got run over, but her party wagon was already moving. If they chose to hop on, what the hell? It was a party, after all; the more the merrier.

Kate never took her eyes off of the darkness and kept the smile firmly in place. She lowered her head and for one brief second allowed her mind to convey a message.

She snarled.

Kate knew both of them got the little gift because she'd allowed herself one tiny moment inside each of their heads. She laughed as she gave them both her back and walked away.

****

"Chief?" Rooba had moved to flank Khryl, and he appreciated the warrior's devotion, but he did not need it. He openly allowed Rooba into his thoughts.

"Stand down, Rooba. She is hurting and angry but is no threat. Our kind has again chosen to break the Law, and we must respect the fear and horror that she witnessed today. The female does not understand her own mind yet and fears she is becoming what the Leviathans call 'touched'. There is much anger inside her, but I know you felt the heart of a warrior as did I."

He paused allowing his thoughts to register with Rooba. "I do not understand what turns a great Leviathan into a killer, nor will I pretend that he is any better than Churel was. The one who calls himself Kretha will die soon, and his death will be from her hand."

Khryl felt Rooba tense beside him and understood that he could not comprehend how one female could *achieve this goal. The Chief looked from the female toward the fire where the men sat pretending to be subservient. He then looked at the Pain Sticks that lit up as the flames flickered in the darkness. The orange glow cast an eerie shadow on them, and both Leviathans recognized the death they would bring.*

****

Kate made her way back to the fire acting as if she'd casually taken a bathroom break and that everything was great. Inside she struggled. Again she worried about why she could communicate telepathically with the beasts and hoped to hell she hadn't finally went round the bend. She had no idea how she was going to deal with this now that both of the giant assholes watched and lurked in the shadows. Stupid, ugly, hairy, stinking assholes and she would be damned if she would let them ruin her revenge.

Both Joe and Dylan were relaxed and even appeared to be sleeping. Kate supposed there was a measure of safety and reassurance for them and the two uglies standing guard, but she hadn't forgotten what she'd heard. Those dumb-ass fakers. The closer she got to the fire, the more she realized her heart had begun to race, her breathing quickened.

Kate was going to do it; she had a plan and was set to execute it. If she could take them by surprise, it might just work. She'd slept beside Joe for years and knew he wasn't asleep; what did they take her for anyway? Kate wasn't willing to wait and find out.

She had the pack and was ready. The minute he pretended to even his breathing, she was off and running. Kate didn't allow herself second thoughts before she sprinted into the camp and dove for Joe's rifle. Kate felt her fingertips brush cold steel and tightened them reflexively. She had the gun and was springing to a standing position before Joe even knew what was happening.

"Put the rifle down, Kate." Dylan was standing across the fire looking at her with a shit-eating grin on his face that just served to infuriate her. She quickly noticed that he didn't have a gun pointed at her and figured he wouldn't shoot her anyway. Time was running out, she had to move.

"Go to hell, Dylan." Kate tossed him a grin and was sprinting for the timber at the opposite side of the clearing. She briefly allowed Red and Rooba's thoughts in just to make sure she was still good to go. Between the two beasts' incredulity at what she had done and the yelling coming from Joe, she almost missed Dylan Thomas's howling laughter.

The last words she heard were his mocking voice as he yelled, "Good one, Kate! Game on."

Well, screw him and his high horse, she thought. One day soon she was going to remind him that the first step off that gloating platform he held himself on was going to be a long one, and she hoped it hurt like hell when he landed. What did her dad always say? The bigger they are the harder they fall.

Kate ran into the blackness. She had no choice but to open herself up to the thoughts of Kretha. She had to be cautious because the farther she ran; the closer she got to beast. The minute she felt him she was going to close the door so he couldn't feel her, nor could Red lead the dumb-ass men into danger. Kate planned on being far enough away from the camp that Red and his stink-ass bodyguard wouldn't feel her when she antagonized Kretha.

The bottle of elk urine was in her front pocket, and as she ran, she pulled it out and sprayed herself. The smell or rather, the amount she used was enough to gag her, for a second she almost had to stop to catch her breath. Kate had listened intently to Dylan when he had spoken earlier about taking the shot when the time came, and she had shot this rifle several times in the past.

Joe had his aftermarket, bought off the internet, magazine loaded and ready to roll, but unlike Dylan, he didn't have the tactical pack or the pouches for the extra magazines. She had sixty rounds plus what she had for the pistol. If that wasn't enough to get the job done, then she was probably going to become mincemeat. Kate refused to let thoughts like that cloud her mind. Instead, she remembered Blake's body mangled within the remnants of the ATV and then gift wrapped with the white metal siding that had been the cook trailer. Images of young Richard, who she had actually grown to like, and the two headless women floated through her brain. Unfortunately, Kate didn't have time to dwell. She would let her heart bleed after the beast was dead.

When Cole and Ben had pulled Blake free, her heart shattered at what was left. His body was in pieces! Kate had turned away and instead focused on procuring his extra ammo while everyone else had been distracted. She wouldn't think of any of the dead, she would get her revenge, and hopefully the pain in her soul could then rest. Lord only knew what was happening inside her head, but there was another task at hand.

She thanked God and herself that she had stayed in such good shape because the only way to get away from Red and Rooba was to run as far and as fast as she could. Kate needed to hide and do it quickly. The trees were beginning to shake, and the ground was rumbling, which could only mean that they were coming. There was no way that Joe and Dylan could ride the ATVs through this part of the timber; it was the main reason why she had chosen this route. She was on a direct path to the upper valley, which meant eventually Sylvia Lake via a roundabout way.

Dylan and Joe would simply track her, but Kate had no idea what the uglies would do if they caught up with her. Sasquatch . . . seriously? She was still struggling to wrap her mind around the fact that not one but two Sasquatches were chasing her. She hadn't even been able to comprehend the fact that Mari and Cole treated them like pets and that Dylan and Joe had no qualms about letting them in camp.

They might be friendly most of the time, but Kate figured she'd pissed them off. She knew that their cousin, or whatever the hell he was to them, was really pissed off at her. For the time that she'd allowed herself to be aware of them, Kate knew that good ole' Red was clearly not happy.

Rooba was a different one altogether. She could have been mistaken as this was a newly developing skill she had, but Kate was sure she'd seen amusement, and could it have been admiration, in Rooba's mind? Nonetheless, he still chased her so that made him a "non-friendly," according to Dylan.

Ahead of her was some dense new growth. The trees had come back thicker than ever after the last forest fire, but none of it was large enough to hide in. The towering over story, made up mostly of Yellow Pine, didn't have branches low enough for her to grab onto and climb. Kate had blocked all Sasquatch telepathy, as she was now going to call it. She feared she was within "Mind Speaking" range of Kretha. The time to hide was now.

****

Rooba was amused and only slightly annoyed. The female had snarled at his Chief, which was not acceptable, but Khryl had made valid points defending her actions. They had not given her enough credit, however, and had not been prepared for Kate to run. She had managed to get the Pain Stick from her mate and had stared the sibling of Merr-ee down as well. The man who kept other humans out of their forest was dangerous, but Rooba trusted him and would have no problems going to battle with him by his side now that Thor was gone.

He paused in his pursuit of her to sniff the air. Rooba could not smell her human scent and knew that she had used the urine from an elk as cover. He had smelled this many times when Merr-ee's sibling was in the forest. It easily distracted the hunters and watchers, and many times the man called Dylan had snuck up on them. Tonight he smelled the smoke from God's wrath; Rooba still did not understand why man enjoyed it so much. The scent of his Chief was strong as he ran beside him, and both of the other humans' smells invaded his nose. They were still some distance behind. It was not their scent that disturbed him, however.

Rooba spoke to his Chief as they ran. "She nears the enemy."

"Yes, I know, Rooba. She has set her course with the Gods, and there is little we can do now but assist. This female, Kate, is strong of mind and body, and I believe she will prevail. Her heart is that of a warrior; her strength reminds me of the sibling of Merr-ee. We must remember our own course, Rooba. Our Clan owes its existence to Merr-ee and the large man who protects our forests. Merr-ee sent us on this journey because the female is her friend; we will do everything to remember that but must not lose sight of the greater good."

Khryl knew that Rooba would have problems with his next order but trusted that his friend and hunter would not disappoint. "Dylan and the man whom he travels with are under my protection, Rooba. Your order is to protect the huntress and terminate the renegade if she fails."

Rooba did not bother to hide his thoughts from the Chief. He was waging a battle inside himself and knew that the Chief spoke the truth, it was an order. Rooba was the

Chief's guard, to step away from his role would put the Chief in danger.

"I will see she is safe, Chief. I do this out of respect for you. You have protected and led our Clan through many perils. I also trust the sibling of Merr-ee to guard you. I mean you no disrespect, but you must see that if you are harmed or killed, our Clan is left without a leader, it is my only desire to see you safely back with your mate and cub."

"I know what you speak is the truth, Rooba, for I feel your distress. Our Clan has suffered greatly with the loss of Thor and Churel, but I am prepared to battle not only as your Chief but as a warrior. You must trust your instincts and those of the huntress. I have watched you, my scion; you have grown and matured into our Clan's best, you have replaced our dead hunters, and your will is strong. Should something happen to me as Chief, you will be my heir. Once more we find ourselves in a battle to *preserve our kind, and I am depending on you. Go ahead now, Rooba, and find the female."*

****

Rooba was at a loss. He would take care of the female and deal with the renegade, Kretha. His giant heart beat fiercely; the Chief may consider Rooba a son and heir, but Khryl had many years ahead of him. Rooba glanced at his Chief and nodded. He pursued the path of broken limbs and disturbed foliage the female, Kate, had left in her flight through the forest. Rooba would not allow himself the pleasure to think about Khryls words, there was a job to do.

Though he delighted at the strong and dependable Leviathan he had become, the hunter within was unable to rejoice. For him to be what the Chief had said was his destiny would mean one thing had happened: the Chief would be dead.

Finding Kate would not be hard for him. She had mistakenly believed so many of her thoughts were guarded to him, and many indeed were. But, Rooba, had focused directly on her for many hours, and when she was deep in contemplation, he was able to see more than she would have ever allowed.

Rooba knew going into this that she was different. He had admired her and still did. Her sense of justice was well warranted, and he had promised her that he would assist her. There was no other course for him now that the Chief had spoken. Rooba was beginning to smell his new female human's scent. He had learned when hunting with the sibling of Merr-ee that the cover scent she used was to lure prey in, not scare it away.

The giant stopped and looked over the still green and lush forest. Small trees grew in the shadows of the larger pines. It was these large and grand old trees that had hidden him many times from the prying eyes of humans. He was going to give up on the idea of Kate hiding within their branches and staging an ambush as the rogue Churel had done because their limbs were so high above what a mere mortal man could reach.

Rooba reconsidered; he opened his mind and felt peace and serenity come over him. He didn't believe they had come as near to Kretha as he had at first thought. But the absolute blackness he felt within could only mean that his human was still close. Rooba had felt her peaceful serenity several times on this day and knew the Chief had been right. Kate was indeed the huntress.

He slowly took to the shadows and hunched his massive body. There was no way he could walk undetected through the small trees. They would conceal nothing of his size and make too much noise as he broke through. The mind of the hunter he had become was on alert and told him to remain still.

Before Churel's and Thor's passing, they had taught him many things; each had his own way of avoiding humans. Churel took high to the trees, as did Thor, but only after it was too late for the Leviathan. Churel had become a rogue killer of humans, but his biggest atrocity was that he consumed their flesh and reveled in it.

Thor hunted the rogue for days alongside the Chief, Cro, Zon, and himself only to succumb to the hunger raging inside his belly. Rooba believed in Thor and still did; his friend was hungry and upon the last night of the hunt, he feasted upon one of the bodies Churel left behind. The sweet intoxicating smell of human blood was Thor's undoing.

Thor had smelled Merr-ee's fertile time, and in a moment that still mystified Rooba's mind, had turned to challenge the Chief. Thor hadn't been so consumed with bloodlust and an apparent insatiable appetite to see the error of his ways. At the last moment, the great hunter had turned away and instead pursued Churel. It was during this chase that Merr-ee's sibling had used the Pain Stick on Thor not knowing that he was friend rather than foe. To this very moment, Rooba questioned whether Thor would have remained a friend or if the large man hadn't done Thor a favor by ending his life.

Rooba could not dwell on what would have come of Thor. In the end, he had killed the rogue and was given a proper burial. The entire Clan had worked closely to see that Thor's mate and infant cub were well taken care of. No one had worked harder than their human Clansman to ensure their safety. It was the human called Dylan who kept the humans away and often procured food for the Clan in times of need. Rooba was a warrior and he would honor his Clan and the humans. He would, however, be firm when he found the female. He understood the Chief's attachment to his human, but Rooba shuddered at the thought of developing such a bond. This Kate he sought was trouble.

He would never be so foolish to trust her in the manner that Khryl trusted Merr-ee.

Chapter Twenty-Four

Joe Roberts was furious. Livid with rage was more accurate. Damn her! Kate had done exactly what that arrogant prick, know-it-all Dylan had said she was going to and stolen his fucking rifle. It wasn't the rifle he gave two shits about. It was the fact that she'd sat next to him and forgiven him for not telling her the truth about these mountains, knowing damn well that she wasn't going to include him or accept his help.

He'd bared his soul and told her that wherever she went, he had her back, and still the sneaky little shit had taken it upon herself to go Bigfoot hunting. Big-fucking-foot hunting!

God, he wished that there were more men in these mountains. Frankly, Dylan pissed him off even if he was a decent sort of asshole. He'd set him up with an outfit that would no doubt take down one of these beasts, but the hell of it was that if he didn't have the damned thing, then he might as well be a third-grader battling the class bully.

Kate had taken off through the timber that not even Dylan's ATV could pass through. It made Joe feel momentarily better when he'd seen the look on Dylan's face when he realized that she'd done it on purpose, he had no recourse but to suck it up and chase her on foot.

Admittedly, Joe had felt a moment's pleasure when he'd seen Dylan's approval when he'd grabbed his pack and pulled out the SBR with the collapsible stock. It was the exact rifle Kate had. Joe didn't think that Dylan thought he had it in him to buy a Short Barreled Rifle in the exact caliber and hide it in his pack for emergencies just like this. Probably didn't even think he knew what an SBR was, or for that matter, smart enough to buy the replica of his AR; that way, everything from his ammo and mags interchanged. Last year Joe remained by his brother's side while they searched for Cole, he vowed if he made it out

alive, he would never be so inadequately prepared. When

all was said and done, he'd approached Dylan, and he

wouldn't exactly call them best buddies, but they had

something in common: Dylan knew guns and Joe needed a

few.

The SBR had been pricey; turning it full auto

wasn't exactly legal either. Joe believed you got what you

paid for, and in this case, he thought the price was more

than worth it. *Hell,* he thought, a man's gotta do what a

man's gotta do

"You're not as dumb as you look, Joe. I've gotta

say I am impressed. Now move your ass; we don't have all

night." Dylan grinned at him to show that he was truly

impressed. Joe was the strong, silent type that most people

just took for granted and assumed was just there. Dylan had

known better last fall when the man had come to him and

purchased a small arsenal. Joe had known exactly what he wanted and knew what it was going to cost. The SBR was a surprise, though, and Dylan would admit it was an excellent choice, and he was glad that he wasn't going to need to loan him a gun. Dylan had never been good at sharing in the first place, and even in the best circumstances, giving up his firepower was bullshit.

■■■

He wasn't happy to be chasing a woman through the forest in the dead of night on foot with another damned killer Bigfoot lurking, but at least he wasn't going to have to babysit.

"Have you always been an asshole, Thomas, or did you just wake up one day and decide to stick your head up your ass?" Joe knew he probably shouldn't engage Dylan in any exchange at the moment, but he was over Kate's bullshit, over the fear, over damn Bigfoot, and frankly, he was pissed off. "Now would be a good time to shut the fuck up and move your ass."

Dylan laughed; he didn't care that they were sprinting through the dark timber and needed to guard every sound. He was happy as hell to see that the man had finally grown a set. He had some misgivings about this operation and earlier had called to check in with his family and Mari. It seemed like his dad and Jack Roberts were itching to get in on the action, but Dylan was glad that wasn't happening. From what he understood, the authorities had already taken statements from the survivors and Cole.

The plan was to reconvene in the morning to search for the Menke's—both of whom were dead. A body recovery would be initiated, and frankly, he didn't want to be around or answer any dumb-ass government questions. Dylan preferred his life as a ghost.

He would do what he could, and then it was made very clear from the start that he didn't have anything to do with this mountain bullshit. Dylan Thomas knew the cost if some unfriendlies found him. Death, and not an easy one at that. He was, and always would be, nothing but a ghost.

****

Kate's plan had been to find some high ground and antagonize Kretha into coming to her. It was supposed to be simple and quick, but why she'd allowed herself to believe it would work out that way was ridiculous.

She'd headed straight up the valley toward Sylvia Lake and hoped that she would be in position before anyone else could catch her. She would not be detoured and knew that Joe and Dylan would be right behind her, but more importantly, so were Red and Rooba. The giants would cover the distance in half the time that she could, it didn't matter that she'd hidden her thoughts. Their senses were far greater than hers, and even with the cover scent, her trail would be easy to follow. She couldn't know that death was about to strike again.

One ridge over, Cody Ronald Lee had found the Preacher's camp. It looked like he was living the homeless life, which Cody figured was exactly what he was doing.

The beat up old red Ford truck was the giveaway. How many times had Rowberson given "Little Cody" a ride home in it? How many times had the ride home turned into a private play time for the pervert? Cody blocked the past from his mind. What was done couldn't be undone. What he planned to do; wasn't going to earn him his place in Heaven, but he had no doubt that it would feel good. Cody doubted that he would leave these mountains alive; he'd left a paper trail with the private detective and once Rowberson's body turned up, it wouldn't be hard to put two and two together.

The camp was a mess, and it was clear the Preacher was not around. Cody took the time to look through the camp. With any luck, he would find evidence and plant it in the Preachers truck.

Cody knew that he was going to kill the man at the first opportunity. He wasn't going to make it a fussy, ritualistic kill. Bottom line was he was going to make himself at home; when Darrell Rowberson walked back into his camp and recognized Cody, Cody was going to pull the cheap 9mm pistol and empty the magazine into him. All he needed was to see the bastard's eyes.

Cody looked into the wall tent and wasn't surprised to find porn and other magazines lying around, but nothing jumped out at him as child pornography. He was more than a little surprised considering the number of boys he had violated.

He was exhausted and hoped the filthy bastard

wasn't gone long. Cody wanted this over with; killing a man didn't wear easily on his conscience. But he had lived with the pain and horror for years. The nightmares kept him awake for days at a time. His saving grace was that when this ended tonight, he knew that his soul would likely burn in hell, but this terror would never accompany another little boy's dreams.

Cody had stoked up the fire, and relaxed. He'd drifted into fitful slumber. Starling awake only a moment later. He couldn't believe that he'd zoned off. What if the Preacher had walked into camp and gotten the upper hand on him?

He sat up in the camp chair and looked around; something wasn't right. The fire was dying down, but the light gave him confidence. Cody stood up and gazed around. The shadows beyond the fire were darker than anything he had ever seen before. There was a musky odor in the air, and Cody couldn't pinpoint where it was coming from. There was no wind. Could it be that the Preacher had gotten the upper hand and was hiding in the shadows? Surely living this lifestyle would account for the smell. He silently pulled the 9mm from the holster on his belt; he kept his back to the fire and looked deeply into the shadows.

His gut told him it was not man, but beast, that lurked within their darkness. He knew if it was a grizzly or even a black bear, his pistol wasn't near big enough. Cody judged the distance between the two trucks and knew he would never make it if whatever hid decided to charge. He decided to slowly move toward his truck which had the keys in it; it was also the closer of the two.

As he took a step away from the comforts of the fire, the brush snapped within the darkness. Whatever was there approached with stealth. Earlier, Cody knew in his gut he would not leave the forest alive. Why he knew this he had no idea; maybe he thought the Preacher would fight back. But no, this was different. It was larger and making

guttural noises. Cody knew it was no bear, and even as the
giant beast stepped out, he knew he was a dead man.

Chapter Twenty-Five

*Kretha smelled the man from the shadows; he hid in
the shadows of the man's camp he had killed earlier. He
smelled the human's sweat and terror and reveled in it. The
Leviathan new that the human didn't have a chance at
survival, and for a second, he paused letting the reality of
the situation sink into the human.*

*Kretha was amused that the human didn't try to run
and didn't try to hide. He stood there with a smirk on his
face and stared the giant down. Just as he thought he would
run, the human raised a small Pain Stick, leveled it at the
giant, and let loose with a volley of fire that landed each*

exploding fireball right into his chest. Kretha wasn't sure,

but he counted eight balls of fire that merely stung the skin

right below his chest.

With a mighty growl, he leapt from the shadows and

hit the human in the chest, knocking him backward into

God's Wrath. The scream that erupted from the human was

balm to the beast's ears. Kretha raised his giant foot and

smashed it with a bone-crunching, skin-tearing fury.

Kretha rejoiced in the smell of burning skin, the

screams coming from the human was a sweet a melody to

the sickened beast's ears.

****

The beast that stepped from the shadows was

nothing that Cody had ever seen nor believed in. The only

thing he could call it was Bigfoot, Cody knew it intended to

kill him. Without thinking, he raised the 9mm and emptied

the magazine; he knew it did nothing but piss the animal off. Animal? Could you even call it an animal?

Cody smirked as his body flew backward into the fire that once held comfort. He knew his soul was going to burn in hell for what was going to happen tonight, but this was more de facto than his mind could perpetuate.

The first thing Cody felt was the giant hand hit him in the chest. The entire thing was in slow motion; his body landed in the fire, the intense burn made him scream in pain. He closed his eyes as the monumental pain overtook him. Cody knew he was dying; he tasted blood in his mouth and felt ferocity toward the beast.

The creature, Bigfoot, was taking away his chance at killing the Preacher. Cody had no way of knowing the beast had done away with the man hours ago. All that the man lying in the fire felt was his skin melting.

He opened his eyes as the beast approached. His eyes grew wide as a giant foot came thundering down on his face. Cody's bones exploded outside his flesh, tearing jagged holes. His eyes burst from their sockets. The liquid of his brain and blood seeped outside his body, extinguishing the once bright fire that had moments before offered opulence in the darkness. The fire sparked and briefly flared once before returning to its resting place in the dark.

****

The camp was dark and silent. The only living thing was the beast. Kretha silently returned to the shadows. He had killed another and was greatly satisfied. Now, he would kill the human female. She was not far; he could feel her. The female was not yet within Mind Speak distance, but he would have her head for killing his only son.

Chapter Twenty-Six

Kate was running for her life. If Kretha found her, she was dead. She figured if Joe caught her, she was in for an ass-chewing, but she didn't care. She had to smile to herself at what Dylan would say, but again she couldn't find it in herself to give a shit. Now, the big uglies were another matter altogether.

She had caught a moment of Red and Rooba's conversation, and knew that Red went back to help Joe and Dylan. Red felt he owed Mari's brother a debt, and truth be told, the big bastard did. It did make her feel a little better knowing that they both would be protected.

If she was honest with herself, she was growing attached to the stinking, hulking Rooba. She could almost understand how Mari and Cole kept these beasts' secret. Almost. Kate had no doubt that she could handle this, and she didn't want to see the hulk hurt. He was a pain in the ass, but she also knew that he was the Clan's last line of defense. This new "power" she had, had left her open to listening in on conversations that she most likely wouldn't have been privy to. Kate now knew exactly what had gone down up here last summer, and it had been intense, horrific, and horrible.

How all her friends had survived was beyond her; she was still infuriated that they had kept her out of the loop. All the family barbeques and the covert looks now made sense.

Kate understood Mari and Cole's attachment to Red and his Clan, and it was frankly weird how Dylan had chosen to hang out in the woods this past year. But a light bulb went off yesterday, and Kate couldn't ignore the people—the friends—that had been decimated in front of her. She wondered if she would see her family again, knowing that they were worried and scared.

Kate had always been different, and last night she had paid special attention to Dylan as he spoke. Kate knew he didn't want to take out one of these beasts, but she had also listened into Red's mind and knew it was the only way.

Kate was going to take her shot, and now wasn't the time to reminisce; it was the time to focus. There was no one out here to have her six. She was locked, cocked, and ready to rock this big bastard's life. If Rooba was near, she hoped he would stay out of her line of fire. There was no way in hell Dylan Thomas would have set Joe up with the equipment he had, if it wasn't capable of taking down one of these creatures.

Just as she was worrying about a place to hide and knowing the old pines were out of the question, she saw something that might just work. Spraying herself with the elk urine as she ran, she caught sight of a downed tree leaning against a huge pine.

It would be precarious and tricky, and she couldn't help thinking it may be backing herself into a tight spot, but it would also put her closer to the limbs of the pines if need be; the log would offer high ground and a hiding spot.

She scrambled up the dead tree, more than fifteen feet off the ground, and was glad to find it hollowed at the top. Kate brushed her trail and marked it with her cover scent as she went, careful not to leave scuff marks. Kate figured it would do little to throw Rooba off, but again, she may need him. It was Joe and Dylan she feared for, but she knew Red would have their backs.

Kate readied the AR and positioned her extra magazines within easy reach. She made sure her pistol was loaded, the safety off, and hung the pack from a nearby branch. If things got too real she would be able to climb quickly, but it was little comfort because she knew these things were able to climb a lot faster than she could. Kate said a little prayer and settled in to wait and watch.

****

Rooba followed the female's tracks easily; she made no effort to cover where she placed her feet. Her smell, however, he was not able to pick up. For a mere human, she was quicker than he had thought. Rooba had misjudged her skills and had thought he would have spotted her by now.

He feared that they were nearing the renegade far too quickly, and if he didn't catch her soon, he would be unable to protect Merr-ee's friend and disappoint his Chief as well. He did not fear the renegade. Kretha, much like Churel, was far too consumed with rage to fight a proper Leviathan's fight. It would be over quickly.

Rooba was picking up traces of Kretha's anger the farther they went into the forest, he knew he was seeking revenge over the death of his son. Only Rooba knew, and was careful to keep his thoughts safely guarded, that the young was already reunited with his mother and the rest of the renegade's Clan. Rooba had slight misgivings about joining the two Clans, but it was the Chief's will and therefore must be done. He also remembered last year when the hunters were well aware that another Clan lived in peace within this forest.

Whatever his thoughts, they were not important now. He must protect the female and kill the renegade or at least hold the ground until the Chief and the other humans arrived. Either way, the renegade would die this night.

Rooba continued to eat up the distance but soon had to stop; he had lost the female's trail. His hearing was impeccable, as was his sight, but the forest was silent, deadly so. He tried reaching out to her with his mind, but her walls were impenetrable. Rooba's instincts were that she was near; there was no place for her to go. The tiny, new growth of trees would offer no hiding place, and the tall trees would again offer no assistance. With absolute silence, he moved to the shadows under a stately old pine

with limbs strong enough to hold his nine hundred pounds,

and with one immense jump, launched himself into the tree.

The forest remained silent, for he was still the mightiest

and, deadliest hunter of all.

From his vantage point, he waited and listened, not

making a move or a sound. The animals in the trees knew

to bury themselves within its depths or find themselves

dead.

Rooba sat silently watching the forest around him;

Leviathans were experts at waiting. Humans were always

wandering about, and it was one of the Rules: Stay hidden

at all costs or face detection and possible death.

Five minutes passed before Rooba caught subtle

movement to the east of his position, and to his amazement,

he caught Kate's white hair peaking from the top of a fallen

log leaning against a pine tree.

He was fascinated to see that the fallen log was more than fifteen feet off the ground, leaning against a tree similar to the one he hid in. Her pack hung hidden in the long needles, and she had taken a defensive position with her Fire Stick. Her body was hidden in what he guessed was the fallen, dead log. She was very well hidden. But once she gave her position away. Rooba knew he would need to cover the log but in the meantime not give away his own hiding place.

The good news was that once Kretha showed, Rooba could be on her within seconds. He had her. She just didn't know that yet. He waited; she would open her mind and draw the renegade to her soon.

****

Kate was in position and now waited. She could smell Rooba and knew he was close, but she could not find him. It was pitch-black, and she couldn't see beyond the end of the barrel of Joe's rifle.

Kate had spent more than half of her life in these mountains, but she was not a professional time keeper. By her best guess and the position of the moon, she'd bet it was between three or four in the morning, using her watch was out of the question. There was a lot of time until daybreak and she needed a little bit of light to pull this off.

Kate needed the beast to step into the clearing she'd selected to take the shots. She needed a head shot followed up by several body shots. She had survived the fire fight from earlier, and Kate knew that a head shot would take the beast down—or at least a couple well-placed rounds to the heart.

She needed these few hours to clear her mind and come to terms with her imminent death. Kate knew that once she provoked the bastard that, even with well-placed rounds, he had the muscle and rage to carry his massive body to her hiding place. She couldn't count on Rooba to save her.

Kate knew going in, that this was it. It was time to make peace with herself, and more important, it was time to make peace with the man upstairs.

This would end today and she figured her life would as well.

****

Chapter Twenty-Seven

Joe Roberts and Dylan Thomas had no problems bush whacking through the trees that Kate ran through. They were no more than a mile in the timber when Red burst through the trees. Both men were ready with the rifles, but Dylan knew Red's particular scent and wasn't worried. Red indicated that both men follow him through the underbrush, and Dylan found himself pissed because Kate hadn't been stealthy in her little snatch and grab nor covering her back trail.

She was good; if she made it out of this shit hole alive, he would demand that she learn some tactical training. She would need it, he knew she was hell-bent and likely had just changed the course of her life. Dylan would be seeing her more often than he liked. Regrettably.

The trail she left was similar to what a D8 making a skid trail through the trees was. Even though the big man was annoyed, he was impressed by the slightly bitchy woman's bravado and even more amused by the actual heat he could feel off Joe. He wondered if it was because the silent man had been taken by a woman or because she had snagged his prize AR.

Granted, Joe had impressed the shit outta him when he had opened his pack and started assembling the SBR. The fact that last summer Joe had called him up out of the blue and requested some guns and ammo and indicated that price was of no consequence was pretty impressive as well.

Dylan actually snorted to himself when he recalled the look on Joe's face when Kate had stolen that exact gun. But in all honesty, Joe was mad but not exactly surprised; Dylan supposed that was the reason behind the SBR hidden in Joe's pack.

Red made short work of the distance; the two men were in good shape but struggled to keep up. Dylan would make a point to share this with him the next time they needed protection from a wayward hunter. The main concern now was Kate and Rooba. Dylan would like nothing better than to launch one of his special rounds from the Big Gun into the renegade. He knew that the Clan hated to exterminate one of their own, but he, on the other hand, had no difficulties letting a shot go from his Weatherby.30-378. It was just who he was.

Joe was terrified, pissed, and livid, there were so many emotions that he couldn't just name one. What he did was blame himself. He should have told her. Why? It was simple; he thought he could change her mind, and when he couldn't, he thought he could either forget her, or the danger was done.

Red and his Clan were protected and friendly. But, damn it, he knew better; he knew they were there long before Red and his Clan had moved to the mountains, and yet even though they'd scared the shit out of him, they had showed no harm.

Now, he raced through the woods with a man he could barely stand and one of the beasts that scared the shit out of him. All for a woman that he would lay down his life for, he loved Kate more than anything and his world had been solitary and lonely without her.

He'd been stupid; he loved the shit out of Kate and had missed the hell out of her. Now she had some weird damn thing happening in her head. She could actually communicate with them; it was all more than a little unbelievable.

She was actually antagonizing another one of the murderous bastards. Could any one of them be trusted? He knew that wasn't fair as he glanced at Red; the giant red-haired beast had saved his nephew and his new niece last year. He knew how much Dylan had given up to save this race of creatures. Red and Rooba and the rest of the Clan living up at the lookout were good.

There was always a bad seed in every bunch, humans included. But why had Kate stolen his rifle and run off like a bat out of hell? All he wanted was to protect her. Did she hear or see something that the rest of them couldn't? He prayed like hell she knew what she was doing. He prayed that Dylan had set him up with equipment that would tell the test of time. She was going to need all the help she could get, and if his gut was right, they weren't going to be there in time.

****

Red kept glancing back at the two men who ran behind him. The Chief couldn't help but remember a time not long ago when he had led two humans through the forests away from a killer of his kind. Now, however, he was leading two humans toward one of his kind.

His Merr-ee would be very upset with him if anything happened to her friend or the big man that was her kin. The big man was one of his Clan now, and nothing could happen to him. Khryl knew he was not to blame for this latest renegade; he was a great Chief and many looked up to him. But since coming to this new land, nothing but sorrow had followed. Yet his Merr-ee and her kin had also become part of his life. For that he was grateful. He would hunt this renegade with his most trusted hunter and pray to the Great Ones that they could finally find the peace they deserved.

This new female was unlike anything he or his people had ever discovered. It scared, yet intrigued him. Communications with his Merr-ee and her kin would become so much easier if Kate would allow it. Khryl had his misgivings that Kate would allow herself to become one with the Clan, though. He could not think of that now. They neared Rooba; his scent was in the air.

Khryl knew that his hunter would be well hidden and to give away his hiding spot would mean possible death to them all. Khryl halted his hunting party. It was up to the Chief to find his hunter.

****

Rooba heard his Chief and the two humans long before he saw them. He could not give away his position until he was sure the Chief was ready. Kate would be onto them immediately if he wasn't very careful. She had a good vantage point, and he could protect her from where he hid. It was up to the Chief and the humans to pick up her smell and to use their own skills to shield themselves.

The hunter watched from afar as the Chief and the two humans halted within the trees. Their only cover was the shadows offered by the night sky. Rooba trusted his Chief to know best. The humans were armed, and the Chief had years of knowledge and his colossal size as a weapon.

Rooba turned his gaze back on Kate. He no longer saw the glow from her hair and knew she had sunk down into her hiding spot. Even he, as a hunter, could not fault her for her choice. His eyesight told him that she had left no trail up the incline, she was well hidden, her scent masked. Now all she needed to do was wait for dawn.

****

Khryls instincts told him that Rooba hid in one of the giant pines, yet not a branch moved. If Rooba hid near, then Kate was near as well. The limbs of the pines were all too high for the human to hide in, but the Chief knew the woman was much too smart to hide on the ground. Kate would seek a higher point. She was, after all, his Merr-ee's friend. And this one meant to kill.

It was still much to dark; he would wait for her to open her mind, and once she opened her mind, he had the skills to pinpoint her location. He had made her a promise, and the Chief would not break that promise, yet he would

not see her dead either.

****

Both Dylan and Joe knew what Red was doing. They, too, had caught Rooba's scent; both knew that where Rooba was, Kate was not far. Neither, however, could pick out Kate's or Rooba's hiding spots. Dylan knew without a doubt Rooba hid within the trees. He could not fathom how Kate could hide within the trees without Rooba's help, and he knew that she would never accept Rooba's assistance.

He studied the landscape as only he could do. It was not long before he picked out the only spot that she could possibly hide in, and that was a far stretch of the imagination.

****

Joe was chomping at the bit; he was a silent man. He knew what people said about him, but he also figured he didn't need to express himself with words to get his point across. It didn't take a brain surgeon to know what was happening. The scent was in the air.

He'd also hunted elk with Kate for years. The smell of elk piss was strong. Red had stopped them in the shadows, and that could only mean that Rooba and Kate were near. He figured Rooba was in the trees, yet there was no place for Kate to hide.

He spent a few minutes studying his surroundings until he found what he was looking for. When he did, he thought briefly about not telling Dylan, but one glance at his pseudo friend indicated that Dylan was ahead of him and had already seen what he had.

The tree trunk that rested against the pine was her only hope. He silently nudged the large man and pointed;

he didn't need to because Dylan had not taken his eyes off where Joe pointed. Kate had not given away her position, but it was the only place. It simply had to be.

Dylan glanced at Red and found his eyes glued on the tree that leaned against the giant pine. It was a solid fifteen feet off the ground, and Kate's vantage point would put her within grabbing distance of a large branch. It would also put her looking down on a beast taller than Red himself. It was not only clever, it was damn near perfect. Come daylight, if Kate kept her shit together and called the renegade, she may be able to take her shot.

What she didn't know was that Rooba hid nearby, and Red, Dylan, and Joe had already taken up defensive positions. Kate thought she was alone, but not only did she have backup, she had two extremely pissed off hairy beasts, a well-armed man, another who loved her, and they all four had her six.

Chapter Twenty-Eight

Kretha stomped through the woods; he was ecstatic about his latest kill. The smell of burning flesh still lingered in his nose. He only wished that he would come across more weaklings. The more he found, the easier they became to exterminate. His only regret was the earlier female. She had potential; he had meant to save her, at least for awhile, but in his heart, he knew he would kill her, too. They all deserved to die, especially after what they had done to his only son. Goya was just a boy. Yes, he had left him there, but he had truly believed the boy had what it took to survive. Honestly, he didn't even know why he was exacting revenge.

The inferior Clan had taken what was his. He didn't care that they were inferior and deserters. If he could, he would kill his mate, Ravana. She had done nothing but sire him a weak daughter and clearly a worthless son. But even she was gone to him now; he could fantasize about what he would do to her, though. She was small and could barely sire him young. He hadn't wanted her for a mate, and it was only at the urging of the Old Ones that he had accepted her. He had nearly killed her during the mating process, and she had come close to dying during birth.

When she had birthed Kali first, he had wanted to kill them both. In fact, when Kali had nearly drowned when she was three summers old, it had been he, Kretha, that had held her head underwater. It was only when he had heard approaching footsteps that he had let his own daughter go, her tiny body floating lifeless downstream to be rescued by another of the Clan.

Luckily, Kali had been too young to know who her would-be murderer was; if only he could go back, he would have snapped her neck instead. Ravana had always suspected it was he who had harmed their daughter, but nothing was proven. It was simply thought that she had wandered away and fallen into the stream. Unfortunately, she was last seen with him.

He cared not; he was the Chief, and what he said was what his Clan believed. He knew Ravana loathed him; she went to the Old Ones and even tried to run away. However, she was the Chief's mate; there was no running away. He easily found her, and it was that night that they conceived Goya. He spoke to her as what only the Leviathans thought they were capable of and told her that if she did not produce an heir, he would kill her. This, only after he'd sorely abused her and used her body for his own purposes.

She was terrified of him and did what he told her to. Once Goya was born, he had no use for her. He wished her dead. Perhaps once he killed the human who spoke through her mind, he would track her down through the other Clan and take what belonged to him. Kretha cared not about the rest of the Clan, but he wanted Ravana dead.

He put the past out of his mind; he was nearing the female Mind Speaker, but he could also scent other humans along with at least two more of his kind. It made him nervous, and he was wary of walking into a trap.

He would sit back and rest; the sun was hours from rising, and he would bring the Mind Speaker to him. There was only one of him and at least five of them. His flesh still stung from the human's Fire Stick from his last kill. The tiny fireballs were lodged under his skin. Kretha wasn't worried; they would fester and continue to cause him pain, but infection was unlikely.

****

Kate sate huddled in the hollowed log. Luckily, it was hollowed deep enough that she could stand in it with little discomfort. Kate poked her head up once to survey her surroundings and would bet her last cent that Rooba hid in a tree one hundred yards to her west.

The woods were deathly quiet, and that could only mean one thing. She hadn't seen him, but it was the closest tree to the timber she had come out of. No limbs moved, the tree remained in shadow, but her gut told her he was there. Kate suspected that he knew where she was because he would have beaten his giant-ass feet past her by now. She also knew that Red, Joe, and Dylan were held up in the shadows of the trees because they, too, would have come past.

Logic said none of the four were dumb. Well, perhaps she was giving Dylan and the big uglies too much credit, but they had to be guessing where she was. That put a damper on her plans. But, it also gave her at least two to three hours before daylight to come up with something. If she called in the renegade and stood up to take her shot, she knew Dylan would be all over him like flies on shit.

Kate also knew that Rooba would be out of the tree and on him before she could empty her magazine. She could not, in all fair consciousness, bring them into this. She was also in a position that did not leave her much room to move if they knew where she was.

Her plan had to be perfect; she couldn't leave the pack behind, nor could she go farther up the tree. They would expect her up the tree, but she couldn't make it without being seen. She would have to use the cover of darkness to shimmy down the other side of the blow down. She had been very careful to leave no trail. Could she possibly go down the steep side silently and get away from what she believed to be four sets of prying eyes?

She could also feel the renegade; he was within two miles. She would never find a vantage point like this, but this was her fight. Kate felt it in her bones; she wanted this beast dead just as much as he wanted her dead, and it would be done tonight, or rather, this morning.

Kate knew her hair was a problem; it stuck out like a sore thumb, especially in the dark. She scrunched herself down deeper into the hollowed log and was thrilled to find that it was burnt. When hunters go into the woods, the idea is to use some form of camo, and in this case, the camo was going to be some nice charred wood in her hair and on her pasty white skin.

Kate got to work covering herself in the black, sooty ash. When she was done, she found a stick down inside the log that was long enough that she might be able to hook her pack and pull it down inside with her. Even if she wasn't sneaky enough, they didn't need to know she was going to make a run for it; all she needed to do was wait for the morning shadows to hide her. When they least expected it, she would be gone. By her estimate, she had about forty minutes to wait. Just enough time to snag her pack and wait for a southwest morning shadow to cover her escape. God help her.

****

Rooba saw the stick come out of the log and snag the pack; the woman must be hungry. He had watched intently, and not once did she stick her head out. If nothing else, he would give her credit for being vigilant and careful. He relaxed into his position. He knew Red and the humans were very close.

****

Khryl had determined that Rooba was in the tree closest to him. The hunter was deadly quiet but had turned just enough to make eye contact. The two men beside Khryl had no idea that the Chief knew where Rooba was. But he knew that both men understood Kate hid in the blown-down tree that rested against the giant pine about 150 yards to the east.

The sun would rise in the east very soon. He couldn't help but wonder what the Mind Speaker's plan was; his gut told him that it wasn't going to be as easy as what they all thought.

He never took his eyes off the tree Kate hid within. The Mind Speaker was clever, and she had fooled them once. Khryl was not a fool, and he would not be taken in by the human again. Her death would not rest upon his conscience; he would not have his Merr-ee angry or sad.

Khryl missed when, just days ago, Merr-ee's sibling protected his Clan, and he, and his mate, Senna, played with their cub, Nyah. Would he live long enough to watch his Senna grow large with their new cub she carried? Who would care for her? Merr-ee would.

He wondered if this would be it, if he would ever see them again, or if he would again lose another of his hunters. He briefly glanced up at Rooba, proud to see that his hunter was focused on the fallen tree.

****

Dylan watched the log; Kate wouldn't hole up in the log, at least not permanently. He was having doubts about her staying put; Dylan figured Kate knew they were all onto her. The group should have passed by now, she would have known they wouldn't have turned back. Kate didn't want them in this fight. She was going to run.

Dylan thought there were only two ways out: up the tree or down the log. She was smart, and even though the vantage point was good, it wasn't good enough. She had something up her sleeve. He dropped the bolt on his rifle and nudged Joe to do the same. There was no communication, but the other man didn't seem to need an explanation. Red glanced at both of them and nodded his approval.

Chapter Twenty-Nine

Kate retrieved her pack and brushed it with soot; she took a moment to glance inside and take stock. She could hardly believe her luck when she found a ridiculous amount of Sure Shot canisters. She and Joe had bought it off Dylan, and had quite a bit of fun messing around with it. It was labeled as the "Exploding Target," and it might just come in handy. She'd blown up enough to know that it was deadly. She grinned to herself as her plan began to take shape.

What she figured was, Rooba and Red were close, too close. She had also surveyed her surroundings and discovered that the log she hid in lay a little to the east on the pine. Her followers were all to the west. If she caught the shadow just right and was silent, she just might be able to shimmy up the log and down the other side. She would need to belly crawl into the new growth.

But first, her new plan: she was going to open her mind and contact Red and Rooba. She would play coy, let them know she hid in this tree, and planned to wait until daylight. She would tell them her plan was simple: at dawn she'd call to the renegade and shoot him in the head. But in order to do that, she needed them to back off; if she could smell them, then he could smell them, too. If she failed, then they could come to the rescue. Simple.

But what they didn't know was that she planned to escape the tree and hunt the renegade. She appreciated that they all had her back because she had started her mission thinking she was alone. But the bottom line was, for safety's sake, she had to do this by herself. Period. Hopefully, they were as dumb as they looked, and she could pull off her escape in the shadows.

It was time to make contact. She opened her mind but was careful to guard against the renegade.

"Rooba, Red? I know you're both close. Rooba, how is that tree working out for you? Are you comfortable? How does it feel having pine needles up your butt? Red, those shadows are perfect for lurking. I know you have both Joe and Dylan with you. You both stink like ass. Do you know what ass is? Let me tell you: it's your behind, where your shit comes from. If I can smell you, then the renegade can, too, and that defeats our purpose. Let's get real; you both know where I am. We're not helping each other if you're all gonna hang out. I am perfectly safe here with ole' Joe's gun. Could you tell him I said thanks, by the way? Oops, I guess you can't."

****

"Mind Speaker, you test my patience. I know where you hide, and I will not tolerate your insolence. I have the humans with me, and your human is not happy. Merr-ee's kin is angry with you, and we shall wait right here until the renegade shows up. You will have your one chance, and

then we shall take care of what is our duty. The renegade

will die. Do not test me, Kate. You are Merr-ee's friend, not

mine; I wish you no harm, and no harm shall be done to

you, but these forests belong to me and my kind. Rooba is

your protector and it will be done the way that it should

have been done in the first place. And, Kate, I do know

what an ass is. It would behoove you not to insult me or

Rooba. We are only here to protect your stinking human

ass. Merr-ee has taught me much."

****

"Ah, Red, you surprise me with your vocabulary.
Mari is a prize, is she not? It would be a shame if you piss
her off and get her best friend eaten. Just saying. Keep it in
mind. I will not ever back down, beast; it is not in me! And
do NOT think you can speak to me like that; these forests
are as much mine. I do not want to get angry with you, Red,
so back your hairy ass off; you stink. I have smelled week-
old road kill that smells better than you. I have also smelled

shit that smells better than you two. You both are ruining my hunt; now I know where you both are. Take my advice: back you're stinking, hairy asses up and let me get shit done, or else it will be a damn shame if Mari has to plan a funeral for your big ugly asses."

****

Rooba snorted to himself; the human woman was beyond anything he had ever encountered. Through the Mind Speak that she carried on with Red, he never took his eyes off her tree. She could not be trusted. But he thought he might like her. Well, just a little bit. She was a problem after all.

****

Kate laughed to herself; she knew she'd pissed Red off, but it was Rooba's silence that concerned her. She expected Red's bodyguard to chime in. She'd even directed a question at him, but he didn't respond, and that concerned her. He was watching. Kate would need to be extra careful, but she was positive that none of them would see her escape as long as she was silent.

Her hiding spot had been compromised; she either had to go down, to the belly of the beast, or up. Kate glanced up at the sky and decided she needed to move; the shadows were in her favor. Silently, as if her life depended on it, she went up and over the east side of the pine and down onto her belly. She stayed for a few minutes, listening to her surroundings and then belly-crawled to the new growth that would hide her from the numerous prying eyes.

Rooba was the highest and the most likely to see her escape. The best thing to do was stay near the pine, because, Kate knew Red and Rooba had the ability to track her. She would make contact one more time, ensuring they believed she remained hidden. Then she would go.

"I see that you didn't heed my advice and move back; I still smell your stench. How can we expect to lure him in if he can smell all of us? I can sense he is close, but he will come no closer. I won't open myself up to bringing him in with both Joe and Dylan so close. Rooba can stay, but Red has to move off. You know I am right. Please, for the safety of those that matter to Mari, Red included, move away."

****

"Chief, the female is right. I can smell the human males with you. I, too, can feel the renegade; he has holed up because of all the extra scents. It is my job to protect the female Mind Speaker and you, my Chief. I do not speak against you, but I ask that you take the human's advice and move deeper into the forest where your scent is not as strong. Stay close, should I need you and the kin of Merr-ee. But Kate is right; Kretha will come no closer, and it is my fear he will double back and attack our Clan. You, out

of all of us have the greatest of gifts to protect within our Clan. Retreat, please, Chief. I know you will be behind me soon. I will need you and Merr-ee's kin."

****

"Are you sure, Rooba? I do not sense the renegade Kretha? I do not want you and Kate out there alone. We have depended on the sibling of Merr-ee for a long time now, and we need him. The Mind Speaker belongs to the other human; is it not fair to take him out the fight for her survival? How would we feel if it was one of our mates going to her death? My gut tells me Kate is not telling us the truth; the female has played us from the moment she left camp. I understand the need to retreat so that the renegade does not scent our presence, but I can't help but think that our Mind Speaker is full of mischief. I know my Merr-ee and believe that Kate is not just going to go down easy."

****

"Yes, my Chief, I believe that Kate is up to

something, and I do not know what it is. I also believe that

we need the help of Merr-ee's sibling if the time comes. I

do not have a mate and know not what you speak of when

you talk of the second human. I feel his anger, yet I know it

is my job to protect the human Mind Speaker. Please, my

Chief, do as she asks and move into the forests and cover

your back trail. I will call for you the moment I need you.

Be safe, my Chief, I will not fail you."

****

Kate's plan had worked; they all still believed her to

be in the tree stump. She cautiously made her way to the

new growth. Working her way silently in the shadows

listening to what Rooba and Red said, Red would take Joe

and Dylan and move farther west into the forest, covering

their scent. Rooba would stay in the tree. He would remain

close enough that should she need him, he might still be

able to help her but far enough away that she could pull in the renegade.

Now, it was time to find a new vantage point. She was going to use bait. Inside her pack she had a bloody set of clothes, the items out of Dylan's pack, and the containers of Sure Shot. She was going to go as far as she could without being detected and then lay the trap. Kate didn't honestly think it would work, but it was the best she could do. When they heard the gun fire and the explosion, it would be all over. She prayed she lived to tell about.

As she crawled, her stomach became raw as the rocks ate their way through her shirt, but she couldn't stop. A quarter of a mile was a long way to crawl on one's belly, but she had no choice; she knew Rooba would catch the movement and be on her in no time.

Once she was closer to the cliffs that surrounded the upper valley and Sylvia Lake, she would feel safer. It would also be closer to daylight, and she would be able to

see well.

Chapter Thirty

Kretha was getting irritated; he was ready for this to be over. An hour ago, the scent of one of his kind and two humans had vanished on the wind. All that remained was the faint scent of the Mind Speaker and that of one of his kind. The Mind Speaker's scent was vanishing, and his mind was churning with anger; he must not let her get away. His own mind mattered not. Kretha wanted to follow the Mind Speaker's scent but feared a trap. He decided it was best to wait for the dawn, not because his eyesight wasn't perfect, but because he would use the time to rest.

The female had proven a worthy adversary, and he had witnessed last summer how the other Clansmen had taken to the trees to hide. This was not what Kretha was used to; he was used to using foliage to hide.

****

Rooba sensed something was wrong; there had been no movement from Kate's tree and dawn was upon them. She should have called out to the renegade by now. He should have come. But yet all was deathly quiet; not one time had he heard Kate's Mind Speak, nor had he seen her head peak above the log. By now she should have taken a position so when the renegade stepped from the trees she would have been able to use her Pain Stick on him. Rooba's gut told him that somehow she had slipped away. He paused for a moment; give away his position to check on her or alert the Chief? To check on her would take mere seconds; if he alerted the Chief and all was well, he would look the fool.

Rooba slipped from the tree and ran on silent feet to where Kate should have been. He gripped the logged and tipped it over, knowing he would find it empty. He spotted the scuff marks in the duff leading away from the tree before he had even reached the burnt log.

"Chief, she's gone. I don't know how or when, I haven't taken my eyes off the tree, but she's gone. There's scuff marks in the duff leading away, but I need you and Dylan now."

*****

"I knew she was going to do something like this, Rooba; it's not your fault. We're on our way. Stay where you are and we will find her."Khryl suspected Kate was going to do something like this; he wasn't angry at Rooba, he was angry at Kate. She had no idea the danger she was in, the danger that she had put all of them in. He tried to reach her with Mind Speak but knew it was pointless. He looked at the two men and pointed, and they all took off running. Khryl suspected they knew what she had done.

When they reached the tree, they began to track her, but it was clear she didn't want to be tracked. She had left the safety of the tree and crawled for several yards and then began covering her tracks. She had taken to the shale,

and it was only here and there that Dylan was able to pick

up her trail. No one knew how far she was in front of them;

all they could do was follow what little trail she left. Within

an hour the trail was cold. All they could do was sit and

wait; even Khryl and Rooba had lost her scent.

****

Kate was feeling the burn; she knew that she had

covered a lot of ground and had left them all behind. Her

trail was hidden, and she was happy with her progress. Kate

had gone straight toward the cliffs at Sylvia Lake. Years

ago, she had found a path up one side of the lake that, to

her knowledge, no one knew about.

The plan was simple: she was going to plant her

bloody clothes on top of the Sure Shot and call in the

renegade. When he was within distance, she was going to

take her shot and hope like hell she either killed the beast or had time to double tap his hairy ass. If not a kill shot, Kate hoped he would be intrigued by her bloody clothes and then she'd blow the bastard up using Dylan's Sure Shot.

The spot she had in mind was a rock outcropping that would provide a rest as well as some shelter. If she missed, she also had two getaway plans. If the bastard gave chase, she could continue up the trail, plant ten pounds of Sure Shot at the base of another overhang, and blow it if need be hopefully blocking his advance.

She needed to be farther away when she blew the ten-pound canister; it would blow part of the cliff and knock rocks, and probably her, onto the rocky shore below. It meant death. But as a last resort, if she had to, she would jump into Sylvia Lake, just at a better spot. Hopefully by that time, Rooba and the others would be there. She had carefully positioned the canister at a spot that would stall Kretha; he would need to clear a path, hopefully giving her time for her shot.

Was it a perfect plan? No, but she didn't have an arsenal of options at her disposal. Put as much lead into the monster or blow him straight to hell. Either would satisfy her and she would have been stupid to get to cocky. She'd pull her shit together and kill the beast or die trying Kate knew that was a grave possibility. God help her, she believed in Him but knew she was on a lone suicide mission

If she was lucky the odds were five to one; not too bad. But the way things had gone lately, she wasn't counting her blessings yet.

Kate didn't know how long she had. It was full-on daylight, so she worked quickly to plant the Sure Shot and her bloody clothes on a stump. She then ran up the hidden trail, being careful to again hide the trail by taking off her shoes and brushing out her tracks.

The bottle of elk urine was nearly empty, but she sprayed the area liberally as she went. She used ten pounds of Sure Shot at the rock outcropping and then settled herself into a comfortable shooting position. Kate had no idea how long it would take to lure Kretha to the lake. She sensed he was near. It was time to get to work. She made sure that the AR was ready to go and the extra magazines were within reach. She opened her mind to Kretha.

"Hey, hey you. Yeah, I'm talking to you, you hairy bastard. Yup, you. You know I killed your son. You know, that pathetic little ugly beast you left to die? I'm waiting; are you ever going to come get me? I've been sitting here waiting, eating my trail mix for hours. I wonder if you're beasty enough to come and get me, or are you as pathetic as your son?"

Kate waited; it wasn't long before the images entered her head. She saw a man lying in a fire burning to death and a giant foot smashing his head. Kate was careful to show no disgust; instead, she just threw her head back and laughed. Inside, her stomach was in a knot, all she wanted to do was vomit, but Dylan's words came back to her.

"Why do you always assume that your vileness affects me? It doesn't. Do you know what a heinous bitch is? Well, if you don't, you're about to find out. Come find me, you ugly bastard. I'm sick of waiting. Let's get our game on. You know what? I have a surprise for you when you get here. You know that simpering, slobbering, little shit that you call a son? I have him. He's actually alive and well, and I have him. You want him? Come and get him. You know where to find me. That's all for now, but if you're not here within the hour, you can consider your precious little son dead. What is it you call him? Goya? That's a stupid-ass name, but right after I kill you, I still really don't give two shits what his name is, he's as dead as you are."

****

NO! NO! It couldn't be; she couldn't have is son.

His son was dead. But Kretha felt it in his bones that the

female Mind Speaker had him. He would go to her; she was

at the high lake that his Clan used to call home. He would

kill her in the most horrific way and get his son back. He

ran as fast as his enormous legs could carry him. The trees

shook, the animals ran in every direction, but he didn't stop

to care or think that there may be humans at the lake; he

would kill them as well.

Kretha was close. He could smell her scent. She

was wounded; he smelled the copper scent of her blood as

he neared. He stopped within the darkness of the trees. It

was still early morning, and the sun had yet to penetrate

the forest floor. He could feel her eyes on him, and he could

smell her blood. Yet he could not see her.

"Where are you, Mind Speaker? Where do you have my son?"

There was no answer; she had closed her mind to him. So be it. He would find her and when he did; her death would be slow, painful, and full of agony for her, but intense pleasure for him. When it was over, he would need to run; the Clansmen would be on him.

Kretha gazed around the lake and determined it to be silent and empty of the worthless humans. The only humans that were ever here were the ones the female brought.

How many years had he allowed her to do so? No more. The giant beast stepped from the shadows and moved about, sniffing the air. The elk were near; he was not surprised as they retreated high into the mountains this time of the year to escape the humans with their Pain Sticks. He had hidden in the shadows many times as a

human had slaughtered one of the majestic wilderness
beasts.

    Kretha easily sought out the source of the Mind
Speaker's blood. She had left clothing behind; he was
intrigued and continued closer.

****

Kate had settled in and watched from the cliffs; she
knew she was completely hidden. The barrel of the rifle
only slightly protruded from the rocks. Even the thousand-
dollar optics and her head were shielded by an evergreen
branch that she positioned to match to other foliage. Not
that much greenery out of granite, but what there was, she
used to her advantage.

There was no shift in the wind; nothing changed
around her, but Kate knew her nemesis had come. After all,
hadn't she called him to her? When he finally stepped from
the trees, her breath caught at his size. He was truly a

Goliath, but she remained calm. Kretha was nervous, he glanced around the lake; she presumed it was to make sure it was empty. Here, there were so many hiding places, and she doubted the beast would look for her on the cliffs. For many, it would be a fool's errand.

She grinned to herself as he zeroed in on her bloody clothes. Knotted inside the clothing was ten pounds of Sure Shot. To disguise the explosives' smell, she had sealed the container and wrapped it in duct tape. She'd then cut the soft flesh of her inner arm until it bled and slathered the container with blood. Her hope was that he wouldn't be able to resist smelling her flesh. It would just now be drying and the scent powerful.

Her grin became maniacal as she thought about him bringing it to his face. The moment he did, she was ready. Dylan would be proud; even faced with something as murderous as this bastard, she was ready, willing, and oh-so able to take her shot. She evened out her breathing and centered him in the scope. He was sixty-five yards away when he raised the canister to his face. Kate knew hours ago that today was the day for killing; she had drawn the line in the sand, and it was time.

She took a breath and only released half.

He was, just as she had predicted, relishing the scent of her blood. The shirt he held and the canister were aligned to his epic nostrils when she gently squeezed the trigger. Her shot was gone, and it was a direct hit. She didn't close her eyes and watched as blood and bone sprayed in an arc over thirty feet in every direction. Kate wanted to whoop with joy, but there seemed to be only one problem. The beast took a direct hit to his face, but he didn't fall. His head was almost completely blown off his neck, his right arm hung on by skin and muscle. The horror of the beast whole was gross, but what was left was something out of nightmares. *Freddy vs. Jason* wouldn't have anything on this shit.

Kate squeezed off another round directly to his head and clipped his ear. Another spray of blood showered the air, but yet even as he roared in agony, he stood. Kate's shot was off by four inches on what was left of his massive head. She wasted no time and released another round, this time straight through his already ruined eye.

Kretha roared with pain, but clearly she had been correct in calling him a dumb bastard as his brain must have been the size of a pissant. Kate had no choice now; she had the ammunition, and he was clearly wounded. Red, Rooba, and definitely Dylan must have heard the explosion, even if they were a mile off. Dylan and Joe would know what it meant. They were coming for her, and she still had ten pounds of explosives at the rock outcropping to stop the beast from getting closer.

Kate briefly thought that if she made it out alive and Joe and Dylan ever spoke to her again, she was going to need to remind them that the .308 Caliber AR-10 wasn't quite big enough.

Next time, she wanted at least twenty pounds of Sure Shot to the face of one of these ugly fuckers. She giggled a little to herself imaging what it would be like to become a renegade Sasquatch hunter. She could do it because there was no fear. Kate suspected she'd been in shock for hours.

No time for shits and giggles, he wasn't backing down; should she open her mind and provoke the wounded beast? Maybe tell him that his precious Goya was already dead? It would do one of two things: stop him in his tracks and allow her to put another few rounds in him or make him rush her. If she got even a few minutes, perhaps Rooba and the rest would be here. From the looks of what was left of his face he was only seeing out of the one eye. His bottom jaw had been blown off, and she had taken out his left eye and part of the back of his skull.

Someone had shot him multiple times in the chest; they were a greenish color and clearly infected. The beast was moving on nothing but adrenaline and hatred. She waited as he stumbled closer. He knew about the cliff trail. In his condition, Kate thought that she may be able to knock him over, especially if she waited and took him to where the last point of Sure Shot was.

If she blew the rock outcropping, she would trap herself, but he would go over and what waited at the bottom were jagged rocks 350 feet below. If they both went over, they were dead. She hoped like hell that after she blew it, the blowback wouldn't take her over.

In the meantime, she had a magazine to empty and had already resigned herself that today was just as good as any to die. She pulled the trigger and watched as every round entered the beast's body. The rage was palpable, but what should have floored him, just pissed him off. She was going to have to blow the cliff

Chapter Thirty-One

Dylan Thomas had no idea how many hours he'd been awake. Was it three days now? This time, he'd been running and playing fucking Call of Duty with two Sasquatches and a crazy-ass chick when he'd heard the unmistakable explosion. Dammit, those were his explosives! How the hell? Joe must have had some in his pack as well. It was at least ten fucking pounds' worth followed up by repeated gunfire. They were less than six hundred yards from Sylvia Lake. Dylan knew that's where she was going. It was the only other place that had a high vantage point. Crazy-ass Kate had either found or known about the trail up the cliffs. Were there no secrets left in these mountains?

Dylan was a big man, and when the explosion went off, both he and Joe knew what was happening, but Red and Rooba hit the ground. Dylan was laughing his ass off even though he knew the situation was serious. He leapt their prone bodies and sprinted up the trail. If she'd blown up explosives, then she needed help.

The closer they got, the more careful they had to be because she was emptying magazines, and that could only mean one thing: the big bad fucker wasn't going down. Dylan and Joe didn't need to run into the middle of a firefight.

****

Kretha picked up the Mind Speaker's clothes. He knew they were hers, and he knew he had been lured here. It had been a trap. Her mind was silent now, as were the woods. She didn't have his Goya. She hid nearby; even with the scent of the elk and her blood, he could smell her womanly human scent. Right now he would relish the smell of her fresh blood. She must have been wounded when his warriors had attacked.

Smelling the cloth she wore on her body brought back images of her white hair blowing in the breeze over the years and the sound of her singsong voice as she talked to the other humans. Why had he always been drawn to the woman? Why, when she had come to his mountains, had he not run her off before? Kretha had not feared the woman until she entered his mind with such rage. Now he held the cloth he'd seen cover her body. It was covered in her blood, and even though he hated her for what she had done to his heir, was it really her fault? She wasn't responsible for Goya's death? It was he, the great Chief, which left his wounded son and so many of his hunters to die.

He could not figure out what was inside the cloth; it smelled off, yet it smelled of her blood as well. Just as he brought it up to his nose to breathe in its scent, he heard a loud noise, and the front of his face blew off. The pain was almost more than he could bear. Had the Mind Speaker's cloth blown off his face? He couldn't think, he couldn't smell, and he couldn't hear. Within seconds, another pain hit him in the side of the head, and he reached a giant hand up to find that his ear was gone. There was a ringing inside his head; he roared his pain and confusion. He expected the Mind Speaker to face him, but his body was blowing up!

Before he could control the pain, another loud bang entered his left eye and exited out the back of his head. Kretha could feel what was left of his eye hanging against his face. He could barely see out of his right eye as it was filling with blood, but the momentary lapse had given him the short-lived second he needed.

The winds had shifted, and his Mind Speaker was using a Pain Stick. He had caught the brief flash of her weapon and the smell. She hid among the cliffs. There was a trail his kind had used for years to escape humans. He would get her. As soon as that thought left his brain, another volley of fire entered his body, enflaming the blaze that festered from the man he had killed earlier.

Unlike the man he'd killed earlier, the Mind Speaker's fireballs went deep, and the female seemed to have an endless supply of them. They entered his shoulders, his legs, and very near to where his heart was pumping out his life's blood. But still he staggered on. He could see her now; she stood with her Pain Stick and launched her balls of fire into him, but nothing would stop his revenge.

Kretha knew his bloodlust would be his undoing, but the white-haired human with the voice he used to follow was gone; he was gone. All that was left of either of them was death. They had brought it upon each other.

****

Kate knew she was in big trouble when Kretha had taken ten pounds of explosives to the face and two direct hits to the head. She hadn't missed one shot, and yet still he came. She'd spent time working on the rock outcropping placing some downed trees and boulders, but if ten pounds hadn't done the trick, she doubted her last ten would suffice. She would wait until he was on top of it and then blow it. She was going to pray that it didn't knock her off and onto the rocks below. What happened was God's will, but she felt it deep inside that it was about to be over.

****

Dylan and Joe made it to the lake seconds before Red and Rooba. What they saw wasn't ever likely to leave either of their minds. The beast known as Kretha was stalking Kate up the trail to the cliffs. What was truly astounding was that it was clear to Dylan that the Sasquatch had taken several direct hits to the head, one to the eye and ear, and half of its face was blown off. Kate had done well, but it wasn't enough. Dylan was blown away; this was his own firepower, and it wasn't fucking enough! Was this shit real?

Kate stood on the cliff trail raining hellfire down on Kretha, yet he continued to advance. Red and Rooba went to go after him, but something stood out to Dylan. About twenty yards from the beast, a bright red container sat clearly on top of a log. Fifty yards away, Kate held her ground, but she was way too close.

Dylan knew what her plan was: wait until Kretha was on top of her logjam and blow the outcropping. The explosive wasn't enough to bring down the mountain, but it may be enough to knock the ugly bastard over the ledge and onto the rocks 350 feet below them. Dylan's only concern was that it would take Kate over, too.

****

Joe saw exactly what Dylan saw, and he knew that when it came to brass tacks, Kate would need to save herself. Dylan, Red, and Rooba would not let the renegade walk away alive, but if they did nothing, Kate would be trapped on the trail. All he could hope for was that Dylan would take the beast out with the Big Gun, or that Kate, Dylan, and he could put down enough firepower to kill the renegade. Rooba and Red had stopped at Dylan's command, but Joe had no idea what Dylan would do. If he blew the trail, Kate would be blown off, too, and would not survive the fall. The love of his life would be as dead as the ugly bastard that hunted her.

****

Kate put down all her walls and opened her mind the moment she saw that Kretha had taken to the trail and that Red, Rooba, Joe, and—thank God—Dylan Thomas and his freaking bazooka had arrived.

****

"Listen up, you sorry bastard, you're dying. If I have to die on this cliff to get this done, you can bet I am going to. I called you here for a reason: this is my mountain. This is my life you tried to steal, my friends'

lives that you did steal. Now, your ugly ass is mine. I've

blown your head damn near off, and in about thirty

seconds, I am going to end you. Are you ready? I don't

think that you're going to the heavens; I'm sending you

straight to hell."

****

"Red, Rooba? I'm sorry I betrayed you. But you

both know by now it's just not in my nature to sit back and

watch as this sorry bastard killed my friends and people I

was responsible for. I can't explain what happened in my

head the other day. I can't explain how I can talk to you.

But you need to know that I don't hate either of you; I

understand why Mari and Cole love you all so much. I even

get why Dylan protects you. I wish things had been

different because I would have liked to been able to

communicate for you and Mari. She loves you. Protect her,

but this ends now."

"I've not been very nice to you, but I am not a bitch. Has Mari told you what a bitch is? Ask her. But for me, one last request: try to let Joe know I love him. And I kind of love your hairy asses, too. Red, I know you have a new cub on the way; I would have loved to see it. I am sure you'd make a great father; you are a great leader."

"Rooba, I think I would have called you friend. We would have had some fun in these forests. The Chief was right; you will make a fine leader one day. You're strong and quiet, just the way I like my men."

"Goodbye, my friends."

****

"Kate, we can still end this; he is wounded. Please."Rooba pleaded with her, but her mind was already shut off to him.

****

Dylan wasted no time. To blow the canister meant almost sure death for Kate. Before he could change his mind, he yelled, "RUN!" He didn't bother to see if she listened, but took the shot on the renegade. The immense sound echoed off the walls of the cliffs, and Dylan saw that it was a direct hit; however, it was millimeters below Kretha's heart.

The beast turned to look down on the group that stood on the lake's edge. Dylan had three rounds in his magazine. He placed another and took off the back of the beast's head. He had to remain calm as the beast stood his ground and roared.

The sound brought back chills for both Joe and him. Dylan had stopped Red and Rooba's approach; if either of them took the renegade on the cliffs, one or the other would surely die. The likelihood of them going over was too great.

Kate had planned this out as a one-man army, and she had done well. He looked to the cliff's face for her, and she had run, but with the cliffs as a back drop, he knew it wouldn't be far enough. The blowback would knock her into the water, and most likely knock her unconscious. Kate would die. Someone needed to get into the water, and there were only two options that could swim fast enough to possibly save her.

For two seconds, they made eye contact, and she nodded her head. Kate looked Dylan in the eyes and yelled, "Do it, do it NOW!" She turned and ran; her once blond hair, now blackened with soot, flew as she ran up the trail.

Dylan had no choice. Kretha was stepping over the logjam. It was perfect, now or never. He lined up and took the shot. The explosion rocked the tiny valley. It was bigger than any of them could have ever imagined. The cliffs blocked the explosion on one side so it only had three ways

to go.

****

Chapter Thirty-Two

Four pairs of horrified eyes watched as the giant beast fell to his death, smashing into the rocks below. When his body hit, there was already so much damage that Kretha seemed to break apart. His legs and arms were all but torn from his once immense body. When Kate had placed the canister, she had known what would happen. The renegade was well and truly dead.

Before the dust had settled, Dylan was yelling and pushing Red and Rooba toward the water.

Kate had known she was not going to be able to outrun the blast; she had ditched her pack and the rifle. There was no time to kick off her boots; she just hoped that she had made it past the rocks below. It didn't really matter because there was no way she could survive the falling rocks and the drop. Plus, she couldn't swim for shit, but the minute she heard the explosion, she was already in midair.

The water approached faster than she could have ever imagined; she turned her head just fast enough to see the beast hit the rocks, and then there was blackness.

****

Joe Roberts had felt intense grief these past months. He had felt true fear, and even intense anger, the past couple days, all directed at Kate. But when she had yelled for Dylan to take the shot, his eyes had never left her body. The second the explosion rocked the valley, he knew; he knew his Kate was going over. He also knew she was going to die.

By his best guess, she was over 350 feet above the water, and that was only if she could make it past the rocks below, and who knew how deep the water would be over there. Would it be deep enough for a 350 foot fall? Or shallow? Either way, Kate could barely swim.

He'd already dropped his own pack and rifle and pulled off his boots before Dylan had taken the shot. Her only hope was that they get to her. Even if the fall didn't kill her, there was no shore for her to pull herself up on.

Joe entered the water moments before both Red and Rooba. He knew that they were excellent swimmers and would beat him by minutes. There was no fear from the dead creature that lay on the rocks; Kretha was mincemeat. The fact he wasn't already dead when they got there was a testament to the fact that these creatures were huge and could take a beating. Kate had blown half the fucker's face off.

Joe turned back to see Dylan swimming to his left and just behind him. He had never seen sorrow on the big man's face. But this was a first. Joe didn't blame him; he'd done what he had to do. They just had to make it across the lake and try to find her. Luckily, these mountain lakes were small, but cold as hell. If the two men didn't die of hypothermia, it would be a miracle.

Joe didn't care; if Kate was gone, then his life was over. Yeah, he would survive and move on. But it sure as hell would never be in these mountains.

****

Khryl motioned to Rooba, but the giant was already powering through the water. He had seen Kate's body fall into the water. Rooba tried reaching out to her with his mind, but it was silent. That meant that she was either unconscious or dead. He pulled himself through the water harder.

"Rooba, I will go to where her body fell. You dive and try to find her. The humans can't stay under for as long as we can. We will need to help them to shore; regardless, we do not leave these waters without Kate's body. She saved us and our Clan and proved herself."

Rooba merely nodded, but Khryl saw the sadness in his eyes. He feared that they would not find the Mind Speaker alive. Her last words kept echoing in his head. She didn't hate him or his kind and wished to use her gift to communicate. Khryl could not imagine not having her around to talk to, or to talk with his Merr-ee. He would find Kate and save her.

Rooba had already dived and Khryl followed; there was no sign of the female on the surface. He could hear the two men splashing behind him as he went under the water. It was clear, and he spotted Rooba searching, so he turned to look closer to the cliffs; maybe she had survived the fall and had tried to make it to safety. There was a beach a distance away.

Rooba swam toward the dark rocks and was just about to surface when he spotted the Mind Speaker's white hair floating in the current. Her eyes were closed and her body lifeless. Rooba was afraid to touch her; he could tell that she was hurt. Kate's legs were at angles that didn't match her body. But more important, he knew that Kate was not breathing. He must get her out of the water and get air into her lungs. His Clan had nearly lost many cubs due to their carelessness with water. He might still be able to save the Mind Speaker.

Rooba grabbed Kate and rose to the surface just as the two humans approached. Kate's human mate went to grab for her, but Rooba shook his head and indicated the shore. As they swam, Khryl caught up and helped Rooba with Kate's body. Rooba felt a stirring in Kate, but her chest was still not moving; he didn't want to hurt her, but he raised his hand and brought it down on her chest. The two human males didn't like it, but Rooba shot them a look that said to shut up and back off.

Rooba was careful, but he thumped her several times before they reached shore. It was the only way. He was careful of her legs and mindful to tilt her head. When they reached shore, he laid her on her back and moved away. Khryl knew the humans were capable of taking over from here.

Chapter Thirty-Three

Both Joe and Dylan knew that Kate's legs were broken from the impact of hitting the water. They guessed that Rooba knew she wasn't breathing, and that's why he kept thumping her chest; a creature his size could decimate Kate, but he had controlled his movements, even tilting her head. Both men knew they had to work fast.

Joe started mouth-to-mouth breathing while Dylan continued the chest compressions. It had been too long, though. Dylan couldn't bring himself to tell Joe to stop, but even if Kate regained a pulse, they didn't know how long she was under. She could have brain damage. As it was, her legs were broken and God only knew what else.

Dylan refused to look at Joe; he knew this wasn't his fault though. How the hell could he know that she had planted ten pounds of the explosive? She had told him to take the shot; Kate had to have known the consequences.

Christ, how in the hell had Kretha remained upright? She had used ten pounds on him and judging by his head and upper body, it had been a direct hit. Kate had set out on this mission, she had assumed the risks, and now they might lose her.

She had acted impulsively, rashly, and outright stupidly, but she had done no different than what he would have. Plus, they had all lied to her; she was put into a position where she was ambushed, and she'd lost all her crew plus several clients. And then, to top it all off, she discovered she could communicate with these things.

Just because Dylan and his family accepted them, it didn't mean anyone else could or would. Shit, if they lost her, Mari was going to have his ass. But more important, he didn't want his friend to suffer anymore.

****

Joe continued CPR with Dylan until he thought that it was pointless. His Katie was gone. He knew she was broken, but no matter what he did, he couldn't breathe life back into her still body. She was so cold. He wasn't ashamed of the tears that poured down his face. Dylan assisted him, but he felt the big man was giving up. He didn't know what to do and was giving up when they heard the thump, thump of a helicopter.

Red and Rooba ran for the trees as the chopper sat down. The rotors of the green machine shut down as the large side door swung open, a man and women dressed in flight suits jumped out. Dylan's mouth fell open as the clients he knew as Ben and the woman he'd been with came running toward him and Joe with some sort of backboard and medical equipment.

Their faces grim, they set to work on Kate. It seemed like hours to Joe, but it was really only minutes before they had Kate attached to a breathing tube and strapped down to the backboard. As the four of them lifted her onto the waiting chopper, Dylan encouraged Joe to go with her. There was cleanup to be done here and nothing he could do for her. He had a lot of questions, and they would damned sure be answered, but there was time.

The chopper took off, and as it did, he saw Ben's face looking down on him. The man nodded once, and then the whole machine was gone. If Dylan listened hard, he could hear the thump of the rotors in the distance. He didn't even know where they were taking Kate.

Who the hell were they? How the hell had they found them? There was some serious shit happening, and it was getting ugly, and fuck if Dylan didn't hate ugly. Ugly meant questions and bullshit.

Red and Rooba exited the trees looking as confused as Dylan felt. It was a miracle. If Kate had any chance to survive, that chopper and those two clients had just given it to her. Dylan knew the beast might be dead, but chances of the shit storm being over were not.

In the meantime, Dylan needed to get back across the water and change clothes, climb the cliff, and recover Kate's gear—or should he say Joe's gear? Then he would help Red and Rooba dispose of the renegade's body. It was going to take awhile, especially since he wasn't going to swim across that lake again.

Both Red and Rooba were already swimming, so Dylan took off running. It wasn't far around the other side, but damn, he was tired. He briefly wondered if he could talk one of them into carrying him back to his ATV. Yeah, like he would ever allow that to happen. Weakness was not in Dylan's vocabulary.

As he ran, he offered a prayer for Kate. She meant the world to his sister, and she held his admiration. She was kind of a badass bitch. That was admirable. He had a feeling that Kate was going to pull this off; he didn't know how, but Kate Mitchell was one tough woman.

Chapter Thirty-Four

The shit storm hadn't been as bad as what Dylan suspected. The clients, Ben and Mimi, were Bigfoot researchers who had somehow caught wind of last year's fiasco.

They had planted a tracking device on Kate early on in the expedition, and another on Dylan, which royally pissed him off. Ben, even though he turned out to be a cool guy and a badass himself, earned himself a giant fist to the face for his treachery. He laughed it off, and it seemed like Dylan had a new buddy. Only this one flew a helicopter, which really could only mean trouble. And it did.

Luckily for Dylan and his ghost persona, it was Joe, Ben, Mimi, and after months of recovery, Kate herself that told the authorities the story.

Last year's rogue bear seemed like a lie that worked once, so why not try it again? Of course, it didn't take much to appease government agents, and even though they were skeptical that a bear could toss a fully grown man onto the bunks of a log truck, they went with it. The driver was made into a hero trying to save the two humans. The daughter of the Menke's was returned to their home state where she lives with her grandmother. Luckily, she was in shock and remembered nothing of the event.

Many of the renegade's kills went unfound; the man he killed in the fire, as well as the two women, simply became carrion for the actual bears that returned to the area and prepared their bodies for winter.

Authorities finally tracked the preacher's location. He had several active warrants, all with multiple charges of child molestation on several individuals. However, he was never found. His camp was abandoned, and it was thought that he was crazy and had just wandered into the woods and died.

****

Red and Rooba returned to the woods surrounding the lookout. Mari would maintain her post through the end of hunting season which was the first of December. After last year's fires, the Forest Service wasn't taking any chances, and Mari never missed an opportunity to tell them that they owed her. Truth be known, she and Cole rode snow machines into the lookout and spent a lot of the winter in it. The Forest Service didn't know that and never would. Dylan always made sure the road was impassible.

Rooba came to the lookout often, and Mari, through communication with Red, told him Kate was still sick. Mari had gone to Seattle when Kate was initially pulled from the icy waters of Sylvia Lake. Mari didn't know how Kate's recovery would go or even if she would recover. She lived, and that was enough.

Rooba was attached to Kate, and Mari always tried to soften the truth for the giant beast. Red knew the truth, however, and was saddened each day when there was no positive news.

Even in his sorrow, Red was happy; Senna was growing large with his cub, and it would be any day now that the birth of his cub would arrive. Mari was ecstatic; she was like a jubilant aunt. She even went so far as to buy silly toys for all the cubs. Mari hoped that Red would allow her into their den when Senna gave birth. Senna and Nyah were as much a part of Mari as Red.

Cole was just Cole; he loved Mari, so he loved the Sasquatches he and Dylan protected. However, he had no such desire to see Red's mate give birth.

He was all for it when and if Mari had a baby, but seeing a Bigfoot birth . . . umm, not so much . . .

Epilogue

Kate spent two months recovering; a month of that in a Seattle hospital where she was in a coma for two weeks. No one thought she would recover, and if she did, they all believed that she would have brain damage. During the time Kate was out, she heard what people said as they came and went, but more important, she heard Joe beg her to come back. She wanted to reassure him that she was just resting because she hurt so damn bad. One day, she just opened her eyes and it was like every family member she had, and most friends, were there staring at her. It freaked her out. In the moments after she woke, she'd searched the crowd and found Joe, her dad and Jace. She grinned at them, and just like that, they knew Crazy Katie was back.

She knew both of her legs broke on impact when she hit the water, and she had a hair line fracture in her pelvis and several broken ribs. Her head had taken a good hit, and they called it a Stage 3 concussion; she would have some ongoing issues with that and possible neck issues. Of course, they went over this with her two thousand times after she woke up and again in therapy.

It was already pissing her off that when she got overly excited, she would stutter or lose her train of thought. What was even scarier was her short-term memory loss; the things she did during that time were not only humiliating but it was starting to cost her money. It was time to put away the debit card.

Kate had nearly drowned that day, and in hushed voices, she knew that Rooba had pulled her from the depths of Sylvia Lake. She also suspected that a few of the broken ribs were thanks to him "thumping" her, as Joe called it. If Rooba hadn't pushed the water from her lungs, and Joe and Dylan hadn't kept up constant CPR until the helicopter had come, she would be dead. Truth is, had the helicopter not come, she would have died.

She had had a lot of questions for Ben and Mimi, but the bottom line was that they were everything they said they were. The exceptions were that they were Bigfoot enthusiasts, researchers, and had a lot of money. Last year, they had researched the events and determined that it wasn't bear attacks at all. When things went sour and Kate had sent them out, they had a helicopter already on standby, and she was glad they did. She was also glad they had the medical training that saved her life. She owed them big time. They both shrugged it off and asked if she wanted a job.

Joe said hell no, but he had yet to put a ring on her finger, so she was still a free agent. She wasn't afraid, and she was going to need a new job. She knew that two months ago, Kate owned the majority of her company but doubted that business was going to be what it used to. Besides, she owed Red and his Clan a debt, and the only way to repay it was to stay out of his woods.

Not to mention all her permits were probably pulled. Hunting renegade Sasquatch did have its merits. You got to own really big guns, explosives, and in her case, she was still able to communicate with them.

After she'd been released, Ben and Mimi had flown her and Joe back to Montana where she was again greeted by all the friends and family that had come to see her in Seattle.

There was still one place that she needed to go.

She needed to see Mari, and where Mari was, Rooba and Red were. Kate needed to know if she could still talk to him. She needed to thank Rooba for saving her life, and she needed to know that everything was okay. She had betrayed him and Red that day; she felt she owed it to them to apologize. They both had never been far behind, and she knew either one of them would have sacrificed his life for hers. Besides, Mari had told her Red's cub should be born any day, and Kate would have to see a baby Bigfoot.

****

Joe wasn't happy, but he had called Cole and Dylan, and together they had helped her up to Richards Peak where Mari was still stationed. Even though both her legs were completely healed, she still had problems walking on uneven ground. The therapy that she went to several times a week wore her out, but even when she was ready to quit, Joe insisted.

Kate didn't know that Joe planned to propose, but he wanted Kate to feel confident when she walked down the aisle. There would be no Bigfoot hunting. She could come and visit, but her days of going after the renegades were over. If she wanted to consult from their home, then so be it. Short of a rocket launcher and a chopper that had heat-seeking missiles, their days of hunting Bigfoot were over. He knew he was talking out his ass, Katie did what Katie wanted, but from here on out Joe would be part of it.

As they neared the lookout, Mari and Cole were waiting for them. Mari, of course, was excited to see family but careful not to hurt Kate. Kate had to assure her that she was fine. After a brief hug, Kate turned her back on everyone, and opened her mind.

****

"Red? Rooba? I know you're close. Can you hear me? It's me, Kate. You probably hate me, but I came to see you. And if you have that new cub, Red, do not even try keeping it from me. If you're close, and if you can hear me, please come up here. It's just me, Mari, Cole, Joe, and Dylan. I promise you're safe, but I really must see you. At least answer me."

****

"Kate! I hear you. It is I, Rooba. I am so happy that you are alive. Are you well? If my Chief says it is okay, I will come see you. You are my Mind Speaker; of course I don't hate you. Merr-ee said you lived, but I must see you with my own eyes."

"Yes, Rooba, you may join me on the hill to visit with our Mind Speaker. It will be a joy to see our Kate. I am happy that you are well, Kate. You are a stubborn one, you are part of our Clan now, and of course you can see my cub. Will you help us communicate with my Merr-ee?"

****

Tears of joy streamed down Kate's face. The smile gave away her joy. "Yes, I would be more than happy to communicate for you. Both of you get up here and bring those cubs. I am sorry I betrayed you both. Rooba, you saved me. Thank you. I owe you my life. And I am honored to be a member of your Clan. Now I know why Mari loves your big hairy asses."

When Red and Rooba came out of the trees, Kate slowly and cautiously made her way to them. They were gentle, and it was clear that the giant Leviathans had just adopted another human into their Clan. With the two giants stood a smaller almost human-like version; it could only be Senna, Red's mate. In her arms she held a hairy baby, and at her side stood another human-like child approximately three years old holding a doll.

Kate looked at Rooba and held her hand out to him and smiled. He took her hand and accepted her hug. It was then that she saw three more figures in the trees, recognizing one of them as Goya. Kate tensed in Rooba's arms.

****

"Fear not, Kate, I have taken a mate and a family. Ravana was the renegade's mate; he hurt her. She is mother to Goya and Kali. They are my family, and you saved all of them. After you meet the Chief's family, will you honor me and meet my family, your Clan?"

****

"Yes, Rooba, I would love to meet all of my Clan. I love you all.

She smiled gently at Goya and offered him a grin. He opened his mouth in awe and placed his hand over his heart. Kate followed suit. Those who watched did so with awe.

The drama was over, thankfully it ended with her life being spared, it had been a shitty few months but Kate was happy, her soul at rest.

Everyone smiled, even Dylan Thomas.

Dear Readers,

Does Mind Speaking exist? Recently a well known survivalist said that what he could only describe as a voice entered his mind and he had no doubt it was from our Forest Friends.

What do we really know? At this point, all of us researchers have a lot of evidence, but it is not enough for mainstream society and for that matter, scientists in general. Scientific theory is based on fact, not hypothetical events.

As for myself, I have been fortunate to have spent 23 years in the woods and have many experiences to reflect upon. I was asked in an interview if I was 'trying' to find Big's. My answer was 'no' there is no doubt in my mind that what I have seen is real and I don't need to prove his existence.

Myself, and the group of people I work with in Squatch Stalker are all anti kill. Live and let live is our motto. We are simply observing and experiencing.

Even if you don't believe I encourage you to keep an open mind. There are many things in this world that live and breathe, yet we've never seen them.

Recently I was asked by a non-believers what, if any proof, I or other researches had. I told him I personally had hair samples, castings and photos of tracks. I told him I had seen it on two separate occasions with other witnesses. He just laughed. I always try to explain and give people a chance to tell ME why they feel this creature might not exist.

None of them have ever given a great or acceptable answer. To this same gentleman, I simply asked. "Do you believe in God?" He replied that indeed he did. I then said, "Have you ever seen God?" His answer of course was

"No." He understood where I was going and became quite thoughtful; he admitted that it was true, there "could" be things out there we don't understand fully. Did I feel "vindicated?" The answer is no, I did not. I don't do this for money or social standing. I do it because I know what I've seen and I believe. I simply want to know more.

If in the course of my life, I am able to stop one doubter, for one second and have him or her think about what could be, I will be a happy researcher.

Think about this:

"Just because something is improbable, does not mean it is impossible." My grandfather told my aunt this when he was explaining what he had seen on a back road here in Montana. I love it and to me, it makes perfect sense.

There are a couple quotes that I think go along with the topic of Bigfoot.

"When men and women lose the sense of mystery, life will prove to be a gray and dreary business, and only with difficulty to be endured." Harold T. Wilkins

I believe what he is saying is to never stop looking never quit, once life becomes boring you slowly drift in a sea of gray.

H.L Mencken, American Essayist writes:

"Penetrating so many secrets, we cease to believe in the unknown. But there it sits never-the-less, calmly licking its chops."

What do you, the readers think? I know that the Big Guy, hopefully many of them are out there.

As I close Rampage and Revenge I'd like to hope you all enjoyed it as much as I loved writing it. Look for book three in the trilogy that brings many wonderful favorites back to the fun. Of course no book would be complete without RED and his crew, they will certainly be ready for the next challenge I throw at them.

If you liked the book I would love feedback and reviews. I can always be found on Facebook as Misty Allabaugh or as the leader of the Facebook group Squatch Stalker. I look forward to hearing from you!

Happy Reading,

Misty Allabaugh

rangrvr@yahoo.com